Great Houses *of* Maryland

OVERLEAF: *An unusual view of Paca House, Annapolis*

Great Houses
of Maryland

BY SUSAN STILES DOWELL

Photographs by MARION E. WARREN

TIDEWATER PUBLISHERS : CENTREVILLE, MARYLAND

Library of Congress Cataloging-in-Publication Data

Dowell, Susan Stiles
       Great houses of Maryland / by Susan Stiles Dowell.
          p.   cm.
       Bibliography: p.
       ISBN 0-87033-384-4
       1. Dwellings—Maryland. 2. Architecture, Domestic—Maryland.
3. Maryland—Biography. I. Title.
F182.D68   1988
728.8'3'09752—dc19   88-22073
                 CIP

Manufactured in the United States of America

First edition

For Brice

Contents

Years ago, when I was making my first acquaintance of Maryland's splendid architectural heritage, I took a tour through the Hammond-Harwood House in Annapolis. I was then producing a series for public television's "Maryland Weekend" entitled "Mansions of Maryland." There was no better lead for the sixteen-week series, I thought, than the premier collections, well-documented history, and architectural beauty of a house that had inspired a preservationist fervor in Annapolis in the early part of this century.

As I walked through the handsomely, and, I might add, lovingly restored and installed rooms, I grew aware of an ingredient in the old building's character that historical fact could not account for. Curator Barbara Brand led the way from the formal dining room to an adjoining parlor which she called the withdrawing room. As we entered the small room, I declared, "This was the most lived-in room in the house, wasn't it?" Ms. Brand's response was to turn back the carpet and show me floorboards worn a quarter of an inch down to their eighteenth-century horizontal pegging. "So lived-in," she said, "that the tread of human feet in two hundred years has worn the floor down more here than anywhere else in the house."

What is it about old houses that speaks to us without words? Ms. Brand's subsequent explanation for the room's frequent use—its comfortable size, proximity to the staircase, and sunny southern exposure—hadn't figured into my spontaneous observation. Nor had the room's furnishings suggested a more comfortable orientation. What I'd sensed, I venture to say, was a kind of patina built up through generations of Harwood family occupancy—a residue of living that still clung to the walls and woodwork and dispelled, for an instant, the distance that time imposes.

This is the greatest joy, aside from avenues of scholarship in architecture and the decorative arts, that old houses provide the public: living contact with the past. In the best old houses, the tales and travails of owners are inextricably knit to the building's physical fabric, and we experience the past as present.

In choosing twenty-one historic houses from Maryland's roster of greats, I've curtailed my selection to those which, in my estimation, have the most socially and architecturally fascinating stories to tell. In my present work as a

Preface

mid-Atlantic regional editor for *Southern Accents* magazine, I have written about a number of extraordinary privately owned historic houses. Here, however, I include only houses that are open to the public. At a time when fewer and fewer privately owned Maryland great houses are opening their doors to tours, the heritage left in our public houses is ever more important.

I would like to thank a number of people for helping me make this book possible. Marion Warren's photography, painstakingly accrued over a period of three years, captured what my words always strived for: the essence of each site. Karen Stuart's staff at the library of the Maryland Historical Society provided valuable assistance in research as did the staffs of the Maryland Room at the Pratt Library and the Hall of Records in Annapolis. The library of my alma mater, Goucher College, provided resources and a retreat when I most needed them.

At the great houses, I am indebted to many people for their time and interest in my manuscript: Elizabeth Harmon, Lizette Day, and the late Gaylord Day at Sotterley; Marjorie Peters and Spring Ward at the Jonathan Hager House; Lin Marsh and Ann Lebherz at Schifferstadt; Mrs. Richard Barroll, Mrs. R. Carmichael Tilghman, and Michael Trostel at Mount Clare; John Keene at London Town Publik House; Mrs. St. Clair Wright, Patricia Kohlhepp, and Jean Lee Eareckson at Paca House; Beth Cole, Dorothy Callahan, and Orlando Ridout IV in affiliation with Brice House; William Darden at the Chase-Lloyd House; John Walton, Cathy Allen, and Donald Graham at Montpelier; Barbara Brand at the Hammond-Harwood House; Lynne Hastings at Hampton Mansion; Esther Shriver at Union Mills Homestead; Catherine Ricketts, "Jeff" Jeffries, and the late Maude Jeffries at Teackle Mansion; Susan Tripp, Mary Butler, and William Elder in affiliation with Homewood; Georgia Adler at Neall House; Robert S. Withey at Poplar Hill Mansion; Nancy Brennan and Barry Kessler at Carroll Mansion; Mrs. George Constable, Mrs. Roger Caron, and Mr. M. Hamilton Whitman at Ladew Manor House; Susan Tripp and Libby Baer at Evergreen; Laurie Verge and Frances Rafter at Surratt House; and Mrs. Harry Hughes, Stiles Colwill, and Gregory Weidman at the Governor's Mansion.

I am also grateful to the editors of *Maryland Magazine, Country Magazine,* and *Southern Accents,* in whose pages earlier versions of some of these chapters have appeared.

Great Houses *of* Maryland

Situated deep in the Tidewater recesses of southern Maryland, Sotterley is a survivor of bygone times. Its steeply pitched and gabled roof is reminiscent of rural England or a storybook illustration of a rambling rose-covered cottage quaintly clapboarded and bounded by a white picket fence. To the trained eye of an architectural historian, Sotterley is a well-preserved example of Tidewater architecture dating to the first quarter of the eighteenth century and incorporating more than half a century of changing style in its growth from simple manor house to country Georgian mansion.

Twenty dozen Newcastle flagstones pave the portico where guests have taken the air since 1750. The view from the columned portico offers a glimpse of the sort of pleasures enjoyed by America's early gentry: a carpet of cool lawn sloping down to meadows dotted with sheep, plantation fields waving in grain, and a majestic sweep of Maryland's broad Patuxent River. Sotterley's river landing was a major port for early America. A legend of pirates killed and buried on Sotterley land attests to the wealth in tobacco hogsheads and English consignments transported there. Its 500-acre plantation was formerly 1,500 acres and is one of Maryland's oldest in continuous operation; five original dependencies still stand. In the garden on the mansion's north side are fragrant Father Hugo roses, Persian lilacs, and a sundial scratched with a name and the date 1828. Somewhere in that garden, outside the long-vanished palings of an eighteenth-century rose garden, may be the unmarked grave of Sotterley's third master, the sixth Governor of Maryland.

Manor houses like Sotterley were built all along the Patuxent River by colonists from St. Marie's Citie in the first flush of their successful adaptation to life in the New World. Sotterley cannot claim the venerable age of those first homes of the cavaliers built in the seventeenth century. Resurrection Manor, the 4,000-acre tract patented to stalwart Deputy Governor Thomas Cornwalleys in 1650, was sold three times before the dwelling that came to be known as Sotterley was built on it between 1710 and 1727. Sotterley can, however, by virtue of its distinctive name, claim a pedigree reaching clear back to England at the time of the Norman Conquest.

Sotterley was named after Sotterley Hall, the family seat circa 1066 in Suffolk, England, of the Satterlees. In 1471,

Sotterley

OPPOSITE: *To adapt his small country house to mansion stature, Richard Plater II raised the roof line on the east façade in the 1750s. In this way, he accommodated more formal rooms with high ceilings.*

Flanking the chimney in the great hall are a pair of early Georgian shell alcoves and a handsome chimney breast. The nineteenth-century fruitwood furniture was given to Sotterley's last owner by her maternal grandfather, J. P. Morgan.

the Satterlees were expelled from Sotterley Hall for supporting the House of Lancaster in the Wars of the Roses, and a family named Playter was installed in their place. In what must be one of the strangest coincidences on record, Satterlee descendants bought Maryland's Sotterley five centuries later in America. It had been named (also owned and subsequently lost) by descendants of the very same Playters who had deprived the Satterlees of their English birthright!

The first sight of Sotterley from the carriage road is all rooftop and gables. Aerie-like dormer windows punctuate an enormous expanse of pitched roof. Four massive chimneys imbue the L-shaped brick and clapboard structure with cottage-size proportions. It is a building that looks antique, the survivor of some vanished, early Chesapeake architectural type. Indeed, the architecture of this 100-foot-long, one-and-a-half-story house is unique. James Bowles, the son of a London merchant who purchased a portion of Resurrection Manor (Bowles' Separation) in 1710, built the forty-four-by-twenty-foot nucleus of the present Sotterley which constitutes the current sitting room and stair hall. His "gentleman's residence" of one-and-a-half stories, four rooms, large windows, and a plank floor utilized post-in-the-ground construction and a type of framing thought to be uniquely American rather than English. It was a crude type of framing, better than what preceded it in the seventeenth century, but not substantial enough to survive two hundred years. Fortunately, Bowles thoroughly remodeled his manor house when he added the "New Room" to the west façade and reinforced the original construction. A portion of the sturdy cedar post construction is visible today inside the west wall of the sitting room.

Bowles owned 1,300 acres complete with dairy, "meat house," barn, accounting house, and additional outbuildings when he died in 1727. The inventory of the "Goods and Chattles of the Honourable James Bowles Esquire Deceased"[1] was nineteen pages long and, from the "Gold Ear Rings" of his wearing apparel to the "11 Whippsilly Bubb Glasses in the New Room Clossett," was indicative of the good life on a Maryland plantation in the early eighteenth century. "Madame Bowles' Roome" contained not one but two feather beds. Mr. Bowles kept forty-one books in his accounting house, fifty-eight bottles of wine in the cellar, and six of his forty-one slaves just for the dwelling house.

Remodeled in the twentieth century, a passage and room on Sotterley's south end are now a formal dining room featuring wallpaper adapted from a design in Brighton Pavilion in England.

The inventory listed 928 feet of inch plank, 3,000 cypress shingles, and 20 dozen Newcastle flagstones at the Home Plantation. In the twentieth century, those very same building materials surfaced again: the inch plank was discovered as weather boarding on the house, the cypress shingles were on the roof, and exactly twenty dozen Newcastle flagstones paved the portico.

How did those building materials listed on an inventory become incorporated into the plantation house? Historians surmise Bowles had plans for further remodeling that were probably carried out by his wife, Rebecca Addison Bowles. The granddaughter of an admiral in the British navy, she was described by an Annapolis newspaper at the time of her husband's death as "the beautiful and wealthy Mrs. Bowles." She took a second husband in 1729, George Plater

II; he would eventually serve Maryland as collector of customs, member of the governor's council, and provincial secretary. He continued Bowles's planned metamorphosis of the simple three-room plantation house; he acquired its title from the Bowles's daughters (all married and living in Virginia); and he brought the estate into the Plater family where it would remain for nearly one hundred years and four generations of George Platers.

The first known reference by a Plater to the estate as Sotterley is dated March 26, 1776, when George Plater II's son, George Plater III, headed a letter "Sotterley Hall." By then, the house merited a title. Fourteen feet had been added to the north. A wing with a dining room adjoined the south end, and the roof of the east façade had been raised to accommodate a sophisticated new drawing room. No attempt had been made to imbue the exterior with smart Georgian symmetry, but the altered roofline gave the house a handsome Georgian mien on the east. For eighteenth-century guests approaching from the Patuxent River for a house party, the sight was suitably impressive: Set high on a bluff, the two-story mansion with cupola, double row of shuttered windows, and columned 100-foot portico, resembled, even to the sand finish on its rusticated clapboards, a diminutive Mount Vernon.

George Plater III was responsible for most of the grandiose additions to Sotterley and for expanding it to the size it is today. As naval officer of the Patuxent, member of the Maryland House of Delegates, member of the Continental Congress, president of the Maryland Senate, and finally, sixth Governor of Maryland, he was Sotterley's most distinguished resident. His upscale addenda to the country house were entirely apropos of his status. That he was possibly buried on Sotterley's grounds indicates, too, his great love for the old place. His life there was happy, and the stories that survive from his tenure as master are particularly heartwarming. One daughter married Francis Scott Key's uncle in the garden on a Fourth of July. Her ebulliently scrawled signature "Eliz Key" can still be seen on a pane of glass in the drawing room window.

Another story from "the Governor's" day concerns a gifted woodcarver and joiner who in the 1750s may have been sent from England at Plater's request to help expand and remodel the house. His name was Richard Boulton, and the story of his work at Sotterley is something of a folk-

Madame Bowles' room was painted Chinese red in the twentieth century but is the oldest room in the house. A closet to the left of the fireplace has a wall panel and shelves that slide out to reveal a secret passage to the bedroom above.

tale in St. Mary's County. A former slave named Harriet Brown heard the tale when she was a cook in another great house in the neighborhood of Sotterley and related it before her death in the early twentieth century:

> When the master workman undertook to draft a model of the stairway in the house, he had difficulty. In the midst of his calculations, dinner was announced, and all went in but one man whose name was Boulton. He was an indentured servant whose passage to America Plater had paid and now was indebted to Plater for a term of service. It was not good form for an indentured servant to be seated at table with his master, so Boulton employed his time while the master was at dinner drawing

A tin bathtub in an upstairs bedroom recalls the last owners' attitude toward historic preservation. The Satterlees' personal standards for the restoration of Sotterley permitted no electricity or indoor plumbing. They used candlelight and an outside necessary.

a model of the proposed staircase. When dinner was finished and the master returned, the master professed surprise at the model. He asked Boulton who did it and when Boulton said he did, the master said, "You go in and get your dinner, and when you return, I will draw up your free papers for no man who do such work as that can be my slave."[2]

After Boulton completed his design for the intricate Chinese Chippendale mahogany staircase (with an alcove ingeniously angled into the landing so that the tall clock installed there could be seen from both bedrooms in the upstairs hall), he was purportedly persuaded by Plater to stay on as a freeman to design a new drawing room or great hall adjacent to the stair hall. The result was a formal room for entertaining, elaborately paneled to a heightened ceiling in the elegant style of the early Georgian period. The building's newfound éclat, born apparently of a fine cooperation between Boulton and Plater, made the simple house something of a showplace. The pair of carved shells in the drawing room atop the rectangular paneled alcoves flanking the chimneys are not only as beautiful as the finest of their kind from the eighteenth century but also are a daring departure from the standard designs of Boulton's time. Altogether, Boulton's work in the drawing room and stair hall are classified by the U.S. Department of the Interior as "among the finest pre-Revolutionary woodwork in the southern colonies."[3]

Governor Plater died in 1792, and his heir George Plater IV died ten years later. George Plater V was five years old when he was left an orphan with the burden of maintaining Sotterley plantation. His father's entire personal estate had gone to pay debts, and he was beholden to his uncle and guardian, John Rousby Plater, for financing most of his personal expenses. Tradition avers that after a series of mortgages failed to alleviate his financial straits, young Plater in 1822 staked his title to Sotterley on a game of dice. He lost to Colonel William Somerville, his deceased stepmother's brother, who owned nearby Mulberry Fields and Virginia's Stratford Hall. Twenty-four years later, ill with pneumonia, he made his way in the rain from his cousin's house, where he lived, to Sotterley. He died on the plantation's grounds.

Colonel Somerville's sale in 1822 of a large part of the

One story from Sotterley's wonderful past concerns the hall and staircase that were remodeled in the 1750s by a craftsman thought to have been sent from England especially for the job. He made the Chinese Chippendale stair rail, and he angled an alcove into the staircase for a tall clock to be placed so as to be visible from both upstairs bedrooms.

plantation brought the mansion into the hands of Thomas Barber and his stepdaughter Emeline Dallam. Emeline's marriage to Dr. Walter Briscoe in 1826 began another century of occupation by a single family. A secret passage between the sitting room and a bedroom above was apparently put to very good use during the Briscoe period of occupancy. It seems Dr. Briscoe was a Confederate sympathizer, and when the Army of the Potomac encamped on Sotterley plantation, Mrs. Briscoe insisted her husband hide in the niche to keep the family from suffering any depredations at the hands of the Yankees.

The view from the great hall windows remains that of a working plantation. Sheep in the meadow above the Patuxent River recall Sotterley's agricultural origins and last owner Herbert Satterlee's efforts to restore the plantation to its original boundaries.

After 1904, Sotterley was used by Elizabeth Briscoe Cashner and her husband as a summer home. A tenant farmer occupied the north end of the house, hanging his pots and pans from nails hammered into the paneling of the early Georgian drawing room. Realizing that they could not keep the mansion in the style which it deserved, the Cashners searched for a buyer for the beloved family home. The Right Reverend Henry Yates Satterlee, bishop of Washington, D.C., provided the solution: He introduced his cousin, Herbert L. Satterlee, New York lawyer and son-in-law of famed financier J. P. Morgan, to the property.

In 1910, Herbert Satterlee bought Sotterley as a retreat from Washington where he was serving as Under Secretary of the Navy. His interest in Sotterley was complete. He studied its history thoroughly and, without the benefit of a Williamsburg or Ford Foundation, he restored it as purely as possible to its eighteenth-century appearance. He replaced the rotting timber ends at the north and south ends with brick, had wide plank oak flooring especially milled in New England to replace the entire first-story flooring, and underpinned the whole structure with a concrete footing. He planted new trees on the grounds, and he acquired more property in order to restore the original boundaries of Bowles' Separation.

Most importantly, Satterlee refrained from transforming the house into an antiquarian showcase. Nine genera-

The west façade, approached from the carriage road, retains the original circa 1710 style of a small English manor house.

tions of families and servants had left behind an almost palpable love for their home, and Herbert Satterlee went to great lengths to preserve the patina of their two-hundred-year occupancy. Between 1910 and 1940, he and his wife and their two daughters lived without central heat and electricity. They used the eighteenth-century garden privy rather than install bathrooms, and each member of the family had his or her own candleholder and candle to light the way to bed.

In 1947, Satterlee's daughter, Mabel Satterlee Ingalls, inherited the property and in 1960 the Historic American

Building Survey of the U.S. Department of the Interior certified it as a building of architectural and historic merit worthy of the most careful preservation. In 1961, Mrs. Ingalls deeded the plantation to the Sotterley Foundation, a trusteeship which manages the house as a museum open to the public for eight months a year. This generous act of Sotterley's last owner insures not only the preservation but also the accessibility of one of Maryland's few buildings dated without question to the first quarter of the eighteenth century.

The springs may have been the original enticement. Welling up out of the ground in the secluded dell, the water ran clear and drew deer, bear, and possibly buffalo to the spot. Legend has it Indians camped there, and white men followed, eager to trade for furs.

When pioneer Evan Shelby built two rude log houses near the twin springs in the first part of the eighteenth century, the dell was wilderness beyond the pale of provincial Maryland civilization. His safety depended on the goodwill of the local Indians—their hostility could make a mere walk to fetch springwater hazardous.

Shelby quit the area for unknown reasons, and a young German immigrant named Hager acquired 200 acres in the valley of Antietam Creek. He, too, settled in the dell by the springs, but, rather than subject himself to Shelby's daily forays for water, he built a house directly on top of the springs. In siege, he had a source of drinking water inside his house the Indians could not poison farther upstream. He also had the convenience of indoor running water cold enough to provide primitive refrigeration. The springs bubbled up from a ground-floor cellar big enough to shelter livestock. The succeeding story and a half, extraordinarily capacious by wilderness standards, could accommodate family, itinerant friends, and the storage of furs and goods Hager's frontier neighbors would come to trade for.

The story of Jonathan Hager's house is an unfamiliar one in a state whose colonial history was dominated by the placid tobacco culture of the Tidewater. Fur bargaining in the forest primeval never figured prominently in the fabric of Maryland history, at least in part because of the silence of those backwoodsmen living at the fringes of civilization. Jonathan Hager left little information about himself, but his house-fort gave birth to a settlement and eventually to an important western Maryland city. Today, the stalwart stone house is a Hagerstown landmark on the National Register of Historic Places, and the wilderness dell is a pleasant glade in Hagerstown's City Park. Although a mid-eighteenth-century attic addition gives the house a look that is more vernacular farmhouse than historic frontier storehouse, the springs bubble yet from the ground in the cellar and tie the landmark irrevocably to the primitive life Jonathan Hager and his kind endured in the Maryland wilderness.

Hager built the stone house-fort circa 1740, presumedly

Jonathan Hager House

Historians surmise that Hager may have apprenticed to a gunmaker in Germany and used his skill to make rifles to trade with the Indians for furs. A dearth of information about eighteenth-century frontier settlement generally, and about Hager's life specifically, makes reconstruction of Hager's storeroom-trading post conjectural.

The condition of the Hager House in the twentieth century encouraged no one to imagine its importance as the progenitor of an entire city. The outline of the original gable of the Hager store-house-fort is just discernible in this circa 1900 view. Photograph courtesy of the Washington County Historical Society, Hagerstown, Maryland.

after December 16, 1739, when he officially acquired the deed to his 200-acre land patent, Hagar's Fancy. He may have lived in one of Shelby's abandoned log houses while he built his large stone dwelling. A survey done in June 1739 so that Hager could acquire Shelby's land cites Shelby's "about three acres of cornfield fenced in and two sorry [poorly constructed] houses" and, for surveying purposes, notes "the said Hager's dwelling house."[1] In 1953, the foundation of a small house was discovered and excavated contiguous to the west wall of the Hager House under the direction of H. Chandlee Forman. It is described as a "very crude stone foundation which appeared, from what evidence that remained, to have been probably a small log house of two tiny rooms, a fireplace, and casements with quarrel panes."[2] Although no artifacts were recovered to show Hager might have lived in the house, its casement windows with diamond-shaped quarrel panes lead historians to surmise it is one of Shelby's original sorry houses and among the very earliest houses in western Maryland.

At a time when most wilderness settlers were hastily constructing sorry houses with dirt floors and windows of stretched groundhog skins, Jonathan Hager was gathering fieldstone from outcroppings of limestone on his land and erecting twenty-two-inch-thick walls of uncoursed stone for a massive building three bays long by two bays wide. It was to function as a fort, a livestock byre, a place of business, and a home for the wife he took in 1740. It was a decidedly ambitious undertaking for the time because living conditions were tentative, and the Indians were a dangerous nuisance. Famed Maryland backwoodsman Thomas Cresap, who lived farther west in his own stone house-fort, found it behooved him to give the Indians one of his cows to eat whenever they called. Nevertheless, on September 14, 1751, they killed his hogs, took his corn, his flour, and his bread with the explanation: "As the white people has killed up the deer, buffaloes, elks, and bears there is nothing for us to live on but what we get from white people . . ."[3]

Indians were not the only threat to incoming settlers. In the beginning decades of the eighteenth century, the white men living along the Maryland-Pennsylvania border battled bitterly over the boundary line. Aggressive fur-trading policies may have sparked the dissention. In 1703, William Penn was exhorting his Secretary of the Province to procure bear- and buckskins because the English market paid

Jonathan Hager's frontier house of 1739 is
Maryland's link to the woodland Indians and
the pioneers who opened the west from the eastern slopes of the Appalachian Mountains.
When most settlers were building what were
called sorry houses with daub and wattle walls
and dirt floors, the young German immigrant
made a massive stone dwelling to function as
fort, barn, and business.

in advance for them. "O that we had a fur trade instead of a tobacco one," he wrote to Secretary James Logan, "and that thou wouldst do all that is possible to master skins for me."[4] The warfare, which was serious enough to detain Marylanders in Pennsylvania jails, was allayed by an order of the King in Council in 1738, then stopped by the establishment of a provisional boundary line in 1739.

Jonathan Hager took out his land patent in 1739, the year a record ninety-two patents were granted. He was, essentially, a refugee from the Thirty Years' War-torn Palatinate in Germany, and he may have been desperate for the kind of opportunity provided by the liberal terms for the settlement of Maryland's lands published by Charles, Lord Baltimore, in 1732: " . . . 200 acres of the said lands in fee-simple without paying any part of the forty shillings sterling, for every hundred acres . . . and without paying any quit rents in 3 years after the first settlement . . ."[5] Hager arrived in the port of Philadelphia on the ship *Harle* on September 1, 1736, and may have departed Pennsylvania immediately afterwards because the English government there outlawed German ownership of land. Although no record of his peregrinations survives after his 1736 arrival and before his 1739 land patent, he could have done what all good German boys did in their homeland: Apprenticed to a trade (and Hager would have had a trade to enable him to leave Germany), he would have taken a journey of several years under the regulations of the German trade guilds to perfect his skill.

When he settled in the dell by the springs, he was in his twenties (if his age at the time of his death was correctly given), and his plan for longterm residence in the wilderness was probably carefully formulated. He chose a spot where the Indians used to camp and where their trails converged to make a natural and ideal place to trade. He may have previously traded with the Indians and supplied them with the specialty items—coarse woolens called strowds and duffels, powder, small bar lead, shirts, and good cheap guns—that they demanded.[6] He probably knew that not even money could buy the skins from the Indians without the requisite Indian goods and built his dwelling large enough to store those goods. The English Commissioner of the Land Office in Annapolis noted circa 1770 while passing about thirty miles west of Fredericktown:

Two upstairs rooms, returned to their original white plaster walls with blue chair rails, share a doorway. A built-in cupboard in another upstairs room was a luxury taxed as another whole room by the British Crown. There is evidence that Hager imported glass over wilderness roads to install in his windows.

A German adventurer, whose name is Hagar, purchased a considerable tract of land in this neighborhood, and with much discernment and foresight, determined to give encouragement to traders, and to erect proper habitation for the stowage of goods, for the supply of the adjacent country. His plan succeeded; he has lived to behold a multitude of inhabitants on lands, which he remembered unoccupied; and he has seen erected in places, appropriated by him for that purpose, more than an hundred comfortable edifaces, to which name of Hagar's Town is given in honor of its intelligent founder.[7]

The size of Hager's house certainly indicates he planned it as more than just a home for himself and his wife Elizabeth Kershner (or Grischner) Hager. It was so large and meticulously built as to be eccentric for its wilderness location in 1740. The entire ceiling in the damp cellar was painstakingly insulated with mud and rye straw plastered over one-by-four-inch oak strips. The walls of the stairway to the first floor were plastered with a mixture of mud and boar bristles. A large cupboard with two doors and four drawers constructed against the wall of the second-floor northwest bedroom was a luxury for the time—the British Crown taxed closets as extra rooms. The Crown also taxed glass, and evidence in the sill and sash of one window thought to be original to the house seems to indicate Hager used glass in the half-dozen or so twelve-over-twelve-light windows. In 1740, when Hager and his neighbors were petitioning Annapolis for a road into their wilderness just so they could import salt from the Bay, the transport of so much fragile glass over the new road was a risky, expensive undertaking.

No miserable dirt hearth in a daub and wattle chimney satisfied homesteader Hager; nor, after the fashion of the English who settled along the Chesapeake, did he cook in an outbuilding to safeguard his main house from fire. In the favorite style of the Germans, Hager built a massive chimney stack in the center of his house to accommodate the kitchen and, perhaps not incidentally, to serve as a central heat source. Practical, too, was his utilization of the cellar springs. His was not the only house on the eastern slopes of the Appalachians built over springs for protection and convenience. A late-eighteenth-century house in Reading, Pennsylvania, for example, has a spring welling up in the cellar that was in use when Daniel Boone was born in 1734 in the log cabin previously on the spot. Hager's house, however, derived maximum use from the in-house water source.

The large cellar, with its four tiny loop windows (narrower on the outside of the wall than the inside to reduce the target area for would-be attackers), wide Dutch door, and standing pool of springwater, was an ideal shelter for

He built his house on top of springs to have the convenience of indoor running water and incorporated a sluiceway in the foundation for the stream's exit. In times of Indian hostilities, siege, or snow, he had life-sustaining water for his family and for the livestock he could herd into his ample cellar.

The cellar acquired a flagstone floor in the twentieth century, but Hager himself built the wall to bisect the pool where the springs gushed. Household duties, like cheese making, utilized one room and pool while the cattle and smithy work for rifle making could use the other.

livestock in inclement weather or Indian raids. Vegetables were stored in a partitioned-off root cellar. When animals were not inhabiting the area contained by the springs, household duties could be performed around the pool where the springs gushed. Cleverly, Hager bisected the pool with a wall so that the springs bubbled up in separate rooms but joined beneath the wall and flowed out through a common sluiceway in the foundation. On the wall above the spring in the northeast room were pegs from which Elizabeth Hager hung the cheeses she made; the residual whey dripped into the pool and flowed out of the house and downstream. On the other side of the wall, ten feet from a large fireplace, the second spring bubbled and probably served as a tempering medium for the blacksmithing and riflemaking that historians surmise was Hager's trade.

Bisecting the pool of water in the cellar created two rooms and facilitated the division of labor in Hager's frontier household. As practical as the layout was, however, the mud and humidity the springs created in the cellar from April to August was formidable. The dampness year-round could not have been healthful. In 1747, Hager transferred title to Hagar's Fancy to Jacob Rohrer. In 1753, he acquired the 1,780-acre Hager's Delight about two miles west where he built a large log house in which he and his wife raised their two children, Rosanna, born in 1752, and Jonathan, Jr., born in 1755.

Either Hager or Rohrer enlarged the Hager House to its present two full stories and an attic. The outline of the original storehouse-fort is discernible in the exterior east and west walls of the house, but architectural historians advised against removing the half-story addition because of its very early date. The Rohrer family's ownership of the house until 1890 helped safeguard many interior details installed by Hager himself such as the full-length strap hinges on all the doors and certain rare architectural features thought to be vestiges of a seventeenth-century Jacobean style Hager brought from Europe. The walnut paneled stairwell and its flat newel post, apparently carved to resemble a human silhouette, are possibly unique in Maryland.

In the twentieth century, the home of Hagerstown's founder was nearly forgotten. The house was derelict, "a retreat for shady characters," according to a city councilman, and almost destroyed by fire. A hunch that the house was old and valuable led Mary Vernon Mish and the Washington County Historical Society to raise funds to purchase and save the place in 1944. Untold hours of laborious research and restoring bestowed new dignity on the building. Now, the plain white walls inside, set off by simple wood trim and chair rails painted blue, green, and mustard yellow, are authenticated as original. A dearth of knowledge about Hager's life and, indeed, about any settler's life on the Maryland frontier circa 1740 presented the historical society with a quandary on how to furnish their landmark that the Maryland Historical Society recognized in 1952 as "one of the oldest restorations in the state." Fortunately, however, archeological excavation done in 1953 around the foundation and beneath the porch yielded a rich trove of artifacts. Information gleaned from the centuries-old refuse has not only facilitated the installation of the house but also suggested the Hagers enjoyed amenities that were in strange contrast to the rigors of their existence. They probably ate their frontier fare of bear steak and venison on polychromed Staffordshire salt glaze decorated in the oriental manner. They may have played music on a German accordian, fragments of which were found together with Indian beads, buffalo bones, and soldier buttons in the debris under the porch.

Today, the house is furnished not just as an eighteenth-century wilderness household, but as the wilderness household of the educated, resourceful, and farsighted man of accomplishment that Jonathan Hager was. From April through December, the city of Hagerstown administers to the house and adjacent museum housing Hager memorabilia and artifacts recovered from the 1953 archeological excavation.

Unlike the early English in Tidewater Maryland, German settlers in the west built massive chimney stacks in the center of their houses. Unafraid of fire, they cooked in their kitchen fireplaces and kept the rest of the house warm with the central heat source.

Schifferstadt

Not all Maryland's great houses are Georgian. Not all are grandiose and therefore naturally selected for preservation. Some of the most important landmarks we have are farmhouses whose startling age and architectural attributes were hidden under remodeling and almost lost through oversight.

By the grace of God and a few local citizens canny enough to consult architectural preservationists, these sleeping beauties escaped destruction. Their restored, or merely stabilized, structures have been revealed, in some cases, as the sole surviving examples of vanished architectural types.

Schifferstadt in Frederick is such a rarity. Preservationists consider it one of the finest examples of early German architecture in America and "probably the only example of one aspect of transitional German idiom surviving in good condition in the United States."[1]

The discovery of Schifferstadt's significance came as a surprise to the fledgling Frederick County Landmarks Foundation, Inc., which purchased the house in July 1974 as part of local efforts to identify and help preserve the area's natural and historical landmarks. The foundation didn't know Schifferstadt was one of Frederick's earliest houses. It had no inkling the architecture had medieval antecedents, and that its history traced a direct line back to an ancient town of the same name in Rheinland-Pfalz, Germany.

Schifferstadt at the time of its sale to the foundation was not a house to inspire flights of fancy. It was not grand like its contemporary Mount Clare. It exhibited no Georgian period panache and no indication its builder was even aware of the fashion raging in Europe and the colonies for architecture inspired by classical Greece and Rome. Its thirty-by-forty-foot stone section, solidly and meticulously built for durability rather than show, was not even occupied. In the twentieth century, the last owners vacated the homely stone portion to live exclusively in the brick wing on the south end.

What alerted the Frederick County Landmarks Foundation to Schifferstadt's potential was an article from a 1959 issue of Frederick's *The News* citing architect and President of the Frederick County Historical Society Joseph Urner on the numerous fine, possibly colonial, features in the stone section. He noted latches and hinges on the doors and cup-

Schifferstadt in Frederick is one of the six best examples of early German architecture in America. Its two-story fieldstone main block was built around 1756 and retains original wrought iron hardware and many techniques of construction reminiscent of a medieval world abandoned by German emigrants in the early eighteenth century.

Some fireplaces have openings at their backs for stoves. One such stove, dated 1756, was still in place against a second-floor wall when Schifferstadt was purchased in 1974 by the Frederick County Landmarks Foundation.

boards made of hand-wrought iron and an ornate iron stove on the second floor bearing the date 1756. A vaulted stone cellar that had a peculiar niche at one end, iron grilles at the windows, and iron rings fastened to the ceiling "may have been a one-time dungeon for prisoners or slaves . . ." Most significant was Mr. Urner's discovery that documentation for "Scheverstadt" existed in the Frederick County land records of 1753.[2]

Foundation members recalled these attributes when Schifferstadt sported a "For Sale" sign on its lawn in 1972. With only a few hundred dollars in the till, the foundation secured an option to purchase the property. The Maryland

Historical Trust concurred that Schifferstadt was worth saving: it contributed a $60,000 interest-free loan toward the 1974 purchase of the $65,000 property.

Almost immediately, Schifferstadt surpassed everyone's expectations. Folks in Frederick had suspected for years it was unusual, but the degree of authenticity revealed in the December 1974 restoration study completed by architect John Milner of the National Heritage Corporation was astonishing. Two stories tall with two-and-a-half-foot-thick walls of rough sandstone construction, Schifferstadt is an unusually large example of the type of house eighteenth-century German immigrants built soon after their arrival in the mid-Atlantic region. It retains many of its original features, which are reminiscent not of any contemporaneous style emerging in colonial America but of an older medieval world the German peasants left behind.

Some interior walls in the typically Germanic layout of four rooms and a center hall feature *fachwerk* or half-timbering, an ancient method of building in medieval Europe. The timbers are visible in the walls, and the spaces between the timbers are filled with mud and straw wrapped around wooden slats. This so-called paling is plastered over flush with the timbers, then whitewashed with lime. (The city of London before the Great Fire of 1666 comprised mainly houses with black-timbered, white-plastered walls.) The mode of construction is rare in America, and very few examples have survived from colonial times.

Schifferstadt's original hand-hewn white oak framing is pinned throughout with wooden pegs, and the roof retains the steep pitch and flared eaves that intentionally "kicked" the rainwater away from the building's stone walls. The chimney, characteristically huge and centrally located in early German homesteads to heat the building's core, in Schifferstadt is doubly effective. The chimney divides in a vault over the second-floor hall and maintains two chimney stacks to the first floor. Off this highly unusual configuration of double stacks are a total of four fireplaces, three of which have openings in the rear to vent cast-iron stoves in other rooms. The ingenious system provides heat even to the hallways in Schifferstadt.

Miraculously, one of the three stoves made for the farmhouse's heating system has survived intact. This five-plate, or five-jamb, stove with the date 1756 cast in two plates is now known to have been made in Baron Stiegel's eigh-

In the attic of the main block is a chimney stack characteristically huge and centrally located in early German houses to heat the building's core.

Schifferstadt's treasure trove of early American hardware includes a rare door pull centered on a second-floor door thought to be the entrance to a guest bedchamber.
RIGHT: *The central chimney stack is unusually effective because it divides in a vault over the second floor and maintains two chimney stacks to the first floor. Off the double stacks are fireplaces for nearly every room in the house.*

teenth-century Manheim, Pennsylvania, iron furnace. Found solidly in situ against a second-floor wall, the ornately decorated stove is the only one known in America to be still in its original location. And because Schifferstadt was so obviously built to use such stoves, the 1756 provenance of the stove is now accepted as the approximate date Schifferstadt was completed. A Biblical verse inscribed in German on the stove translates: "Where your treasure is, there will your heart be also," establishing an invaluable link to those persecuted Germans who came to Maryland with little more than religion, husbandry, and a centuries-old way of heating with stove *ofens.*

Elsewhere in the old stone section, the hardware on doors and cupboards has been verified as a treasure trove of early American wrought ironwork. Elaborate latches, escutcheon plates, and hinges are well preserved, including a rare door pull centered on a second-floor door thought to be the entrance to the bedroom reserved for guests. Ram's horn side hinges on a small bedroom wall cabinet look distinctly Old World and slightly the worse for wear. As is the intention at Schifferstadt, however, the more-than-two-centuries-old "Bible cabinet" has not been restored, merely stabilized along with the rest of the architecture in order to focus attention on the building's incomparable degree of originality.

The part of Schifferstadt that inspired legend and piqued every local boy's curiosity was the "dungeon." According to Milner's study, the vaulted stone room under the house with iron rings in the ceiling and grilles at the ground-level windows is a German *keller* or cellar. Resting on bedrock, it was laboriously hand excavated by its German builder to provide both a foundation for the stone house and a year-round cool place for food storage. Cured meats, not incarcerated slaves, were tied to the big iron ceiling rings, and the iron grillework on the big vents to the outside kept animal and human marauders from the stores of fruit, vegetables, sauerkraut, beer, and wine below. The large niche in one wall is now known not to conceal a tunnel as was previously believed. Its function has not been determined, but the discovery of similar cellar niches in medieval houses in Schifferstadt, Germany, has provided a new avenue of research on the peculiar architectural element.

Schifferstadt's connection with Schifferstadt, Germany, is at least as intriguing as its architecture. The Frederick County Landmarks Foundation established the link between the Joseph Brunner who owned "Scheverstadt" in Frederick County in 1753 and the Joseph Brunner who was married in the village of Klein-Schifferstadt near Mannheim, Germany, in 1700, manumitted in April 1729, and listed with his wife Catharina Elisabetha and five of his six children as passengers aboard the *Allen* arriving in Philadelphia on September 15, 1729. The supposition is that Brunner, in reduced circumstances like hundreds of thousands of other Germans in the war-torn Palatinate, immigrated to the "neue Land" to take advantage of William Penn's well-advertised, liberal land settlement policies in America. Unlike most of his émigré brethren, however, when Brunner left his home (whose population of 684 in

Some sophistication of construction is apparent in the regular coursing of the fieldstone in the front façade and in the handsome stone relieving arches above the door and window openings.

Walls in the parlor were replastered in the twentieth century but elsewhere in the house exhibit a type of medieval German construction called fachwerk *that is the first example of its kind found in Maryland.*

the seventeenth century was reduced to fifteen by the Thirty Years War and the bubonic plague), he didn't blot it from memory.

He and his oldest son Jacob, who preceded him to America by one year, eventually brought their families to Maryland where land could be rented free for the first three years and for a penny an acre thereafter. There, in Frederickstadt, in the valley of the Monocacy River, Joseph Brunner, formerly a peasant with no landowning privileges, purchased land from his English landlord. No whimsical, vacuous, or English appellation suited this proud German. He named his homestead Scheverstadt for the place in Europe he had abandoned but, apparently, did not want to forget.

The odds had been against Brunner and his sons acquiring English colonial land. They had little money, little

The foundation maintains Schifferstadt as an architectural museum. Stabilized, unadorned interiors such as the kitchen emphasize the building's rare architectural features.

understanding of the English language, and, because of a Germanic tradition of serfdom, were not inclined to try to buy the land they rented. Most of the western Maryland frontier had been purchased for investment by wealthy Annapolitans, and those gentlemen were not wont to divest themselves of a German tenantry industriously applying thirty generations of farming knowledge to raw wilderness. What's more, many English colonials disliked people they considered stupid and actually called Palatine boors, and, by placing legal restrictions on how the Germans could own land, were able, without compunction, to exploit them.

One English gentleman, however, would not exploit the Germans. Daniel Dulaney, a barrister in the Maryland Tidewater region, purchased the 7,000-acre Tasker's Chance under the strict condition that those people already settled there could purchase their rented portions from him. The Brunners had been in the "Monocasie" at least since 1736 when two of the Brunner women took part in a local baptism. Joseph and his sons had signed the 1742 petition to divide the county and were listed on the rent rolls of 1744. With alacrity, they must have accepted Dulaney's offer of land ownership.

On July 28, 1746, for a consideration of £10, Joseph Brunner received a deed for the 303 acres he was farming north of the newly laid out town of Frederickstadt. Very probably, £10 was not the full purchase price but a lease arrangement with Dulaney who was known to give deeds to his tenant farmers on Tasker's Chance at whatever time they were able to finish paying him. Brunner's three sons and a son-in-law also received deeds for parcels they had been farming nearby.

There is no mention of a house on Joseph's property in the deed of 1746; nor does the deed of 1753, in which Joseph sold Scheverstadt to his youngest son Elias for £200, note any buildings. Perhaps Joseph's first house in the wilderness was not significant enough to mention and no longer exists. Schifferstadt was possibly the second house on the property, the product of a second, more-settled generation of Germans substituting stone for the log construction of their land-clearing fathers' generation. Certainly, the great difference between the £200 Elias paid for the property in 1753 and the £1,500 he sold it for in 1771 seems to indicate he made a large improvement. That large improvement—the house Schifferstadt—was probably built circa 1756, for, having built the house to accommodate cast iron stoves, he would have purchased and installed his 1756 *ofen* as soon as possible after finishing the house.

Elias Brunner, farmer, sold his 303 acres with "buildings and improvements" to his nephew by marriage, Christopher Meyer, in 1771. Meyer willed the farm to his sons John and Israel in 1812, and it was during Israel's post-1812 tenancy that most of the changes, including the addition of a brick wing, were made to the house. To date, the earliest detailed list of the contents of Schifferstadt was made on the death of Israel Meyer in 1842. Earlier probate inventories have been found for Joseph Brunner's neighbors and his sons, but none has yet come to light listing Schifferstadt's household contents in the eighteenth century.

Schifferstadt passed from Joseph Brunner's relatives in 1843 to Christian Steiner, whose son Lewis sold it in 1900 to Edward Krantz. The Krantz family unknowingly helped preserve the old stone section by abandoning it for living quarters in the brick wing. Only three families lived in Schifferstadt, but in that time—ten generations—any inherited knowledge of the building's beginnings had faded from memory. What's more, a dearth of similar structures from early Frederick eliminated the possibility of helpful local comparison.

Sharp-eyed antiquarians, resorting to picking paint layers off walls and exploring eighteenth-century structures in Pennsylvania Dutch country, made the first breakthroughs. Their coup was the serendipitous rediscovery of the stone sink for the kitchen. It was found propped up against the back of the house as a makeshift drain. The concerted efforts of a host of volunteers in the Frederick County Landmarks Foundation facilitated Schifferstadt's restoration, and today their continued efforts are united in maintaining the building as an architectural museum. The lack of furnishings in Schifferstadt's unenhanced, stabilized interiors draws attention to its rare architecture and serves, also, to warn visitors what the dulling hand of time could otherwise hide from incurious eyes.

Schifferstadt's function today is educational. Through the Smithsonian Institution, the Historic House Association conducted workshops in restoration techniques on the premises in 1979. Self-guided tours of Schifferstadt's architectural features also introduce the public to the lifestyle and role of German immigrants in early American culture. First to irrigate, rotate crops, and recycle manure, the assiduous German farmer was an indispensable supplier of foodstuffs during the French and Indian, and Revolutionary wars. For too long his contributions, including his solidly crafted, centrally heated vernacular architecture, have been overlooked. In the fortuitous restoration of Schifferstadt, America has acquired an appropriate memorial to the German colonist.

ABOVE: *Fitted under a kitchen window is a stone sink that was used to channel water under the sill and out of the kitchen through a chute chiseled in the stone.*

BELOW: *The massive stone sink had been removed prior to Schifferstadt's restoration but was rediscovered propped against the house as a makeshift drain.*

Mount Clare

The "wild geese" of Ely O'Carroll flew far from Ireland after the loss of their hereditary lands to the English in the seventeenth century. Two of these disaffected sons of ancient Irish lineage landed on provincial Maryland shores to establish financial empires rivaling any birthright denied them in the Old World.

Both men were distantly related progeny of the thirteenth-century Prince Teige O'Carroll of Ely, and both were named Charles Carroll. They immigrated within twenty-seven years of each other to Annapolis. Charles Carroll "the settler" and Charles Carroll "the doctor" made fortunes in land speculation and business enterprises. They married in Maryland, lived comfortably, and named their firstborn sons Charles.

It is with Dr. Carroll's family that the architectural prototype originated for the most sophisticated houses of eighteenth-century Maryland. Called Mount Clare or "The Mount" by the Carrolls, it was among the first country seats built by Maryland's gentry primarily for pleasurable rather than working use. The architecture was one of the first to introduce to the colonies a concept popular in England beginning in the mideighteenth century: the country house composition by Italian architect Andrea Palladio of a villa with attached wings ending in pavilions. New and innovative elements of style appealed to the fashion-conscious Carrolls while providing a foundation for Maryland's finest architecture.

Mount Clare did not spring 350 feet and fully formed on its scenic hilltop above the Patapsco River and fledgling Baltimore Town as the brainchild of a single colonial architectural intelligence. The modest antecedent of this mansion was a one-and-a-half-story clapboard "house 50 feet long 20 feet wide, stack of chimneys with 4 fire places"[1] erected by Dr. Carroll circa 1749-1751. Seventeen years earlier, the doctor had purchased 2,368 acres of land which he named "Georgia" on tributaries of the Patapsco River in Baltimore County. The discovery of high-grade iron ore on the tract and subsequent development of the Baltimore Iron Works and peripheral planting, milling, and shipping enterprises required his presence often in the area. The small plantation house may have been built for his family's use when they accompanied him from their primary residence in Annapolis to the undeveloped country of the upper Chesapeake Bay.

OPPOSITE: *Mrs. Carroll's fire screen and suite of ten white and gold Louis XV chairs and sofa remain in the parlor. The barrister's order for furnishings in Europe included "Turkey carpets, mirrors with gilt frames, dressing tables of mahogany and heppelwhite chairs." Copies of his original orders still exist.*

The Palladian window on Mount Clare's front façade is one of the first made for a Maryland residence. It was incorporated into a portico with marble pavings and limestone columns ordered from England and added to the main block in 1767.

In 1753, the ambitious doctor was contemplating settling his younger son, John Henry Carroll, on the property "at Patapsco to build a Merchant Mill there; and make it a Center for my Business . . ."[2] In 1754, however, his twenty-two-year-old son died of consumption, and a year later, Dr. Carroll died at the age of sixty-four. Whether young "Jackie" ever made the modest frame house his bachelor quarters is not known, but elder brother Charles Carroll's return from sixteen years of education at Europe's finest institutions seems to have initiated in 1756 the construction of a large, new building on the site.

Charles Carroll, distinguished from others of that name in Maryland by his title Barrister-at-Law, inherited the bulk of his father's massive estate. An education, begun at the age of ten, at the English House in Lisbon, Eton, Cambridge University, and the Inns of Court in London not only prepared him to practice law in the colonies, but also to further his father's multiple business interests. At thirty-three years old, and among the wealthiest men in Maryland, Charles Carroll, Barrister, placed an order to England for nails, hardware, sheet lead, and window glass. He may have been fulfilling his father's wistful yearning to establish a more substantial seat near the family's major business holdings or simply setting himself up in the civilized manner to which he'd grown accustomed in London. Whatever the motivation, the initial order for the new house in the summer of 1756 bespoke confidence and careful planning: the windows would be of two different sizes and require 701 pieces of glass!

Given the absence in the twentieth century of any traces of a foundation from the early frame structure, archeologists have deduced that Charles Carroll, Barrister, may have dismantled the first house and built the main block or the kitchen wing of the new structure over top its foundation.[3] He might have recycled the hardware and building materials from the earlier building as well. Mount Clare's construction can be said to span the period from the 1756 date of the barrister's first order for British-made building materials, at which time the plans for the house would have been finalized, to 1760 when another order to London enumerated furnishings such as Turkey carpets and looking glasses for a house, presumably the new house. His correspondence indicates he was living in his house in Baltimore County in 1760 and referring to it as Mount Clare after

A nineteenth-century Baltimore card table picturing Mount Clare in the eighteenth century helped architectural historians return the house to its original configuration.

1760. Clare was a feminine name of sentimental significance in the Carroll family. Dr. Carroll's mother, whom he left in Ireland circa 1715, was Clare Dunn. The barrister's sister was Mary Clare, and his daughter who died before the age of two was Margaret Clare.

Although the architect for the hilltop house has yet to be determined, the basic floor plan could have been taken from several pattern books of the 1750s. Mount Clare's initial manifestation as a main block and one (kitchen) wing was a rather severe model of mid-Georgian rectitude notable for the irregular Flemish bond of its brick walls not found on any other Maryland buildings of the time. Four massive brick pilasters handsomely inset with glazed header bricks span the garden façade and recall the architecture of seventeenth-century England. A panoramic landscape painted by Charles Willson Peale in 1775 of Mount Clare on its garden acreage shows the monumental effect of the big pilasters and center pediment from a distance. Ships heading up the Middle Branch of the Patapsco River to the barrister's wharves would have been less taken with the meager settlement on shore spawned by the iron trade than with the pristine country house overlooking the long riverine avenue from the Chesapeake Bay.

By 1763, Carroll was no longer paying taxes for his bachelor status: he married Margaret Tilghman, a cousin from Talbot County nineteen years his junior. Carroll's orders for English goods in the early years of his marriage disclose sophisticated tastes and ample funds. His awareness of current trends, particularly of the flurry of building in Annapolis in the new Palladian style, probably inspired his enlargement of Mount Clare.

Very simply, the additions Carroll made in 1766 and 1767 were a wing on the west to balance the extant kitchen wing on the east, a hyphen connecting it to the main block, and a portico incorporating a second-story boudoir that framed the front entry of the main block. Viewed as an entity, the new Mount Clare was a rhythmic modulation of masses using a number of graceful new architectural motifs that only a highly skilled architect would have been familiar with. No eighteenth-century document as yet has revealed the identity of Mount Clare's architect at this stage, but his motifs reappear in Maryland's great Georgian style houses as semi-octagonal wing ends, ogee arched hyphens,

and columned porches surmounted by lovely Palladian windows.

From the front or north façade, Mount Clare suggested compactness and sophistication. As seen on a Federal card table decorated with a painting of the house in the early nineteenth century, the original exterior included a broad walkway up to the house and a carriage drive outside a courtyard. Recent archeological investigation by the Baltimore Center for Urban Archeology has enabled restoration of the semicircular wall and gate piers framing Mount Clare at the end of its access road from the public highway. Future archeological investigation will aid in the restoration

When Baltimore was a town of barely 500, Dr. Charles Carroll was planning the country house he named after his mother in Ireland on 800 acres of Patapsco River land he called Georgia Plantation. Two sons lived on the property after him, but son Charles, a barrister-at-law educated in Europe, completed the fine Georgian house with white stone imported from England and pink brick fired from Baltimore clay.

Mr. and Mrs. Carroll's own cradles, treasured by descendants, recall the couple's twin children who died in infancy.

of Mount Clare's garden or south façade with outbuildings such as the wash house, ice house, shed, and orangerie that extended 350 feet along a manicured bowling green at the top of the hill.

Mount Clare's gardens were among the most extensive and beautiful of the time. A series of grass terraces that descended to fields and pastures along the Patapsco River, a mile away, were picturesque enough to merit description in several period diaries. John Adams described his impressions of a walk he took while in Baltimore for the Continental Congress of 1777:

> At the Point you have a full view of the elegant, splendid Seat of Mr. Carroll Barrister. It is a large and elegant House. It stands fronting and looking down the River, into the Harbour. It is one Mile from the Water. There is a most beautifull Walk from the House down to the Water. There is a descent, not far from the House. You have a fine garden—then you descend a few Steps and have another fine Garden—you go down a few more and have another. It is now the dead of Winter, no Verdure, or bloom to be seen, but in the Spring, Summer, and Fall this Scaene must be very pretty.

The National Society of the Colonial Dames of America in the State of Maryland have maintained Mount Clare as a museum since 1917. They have located, documented, and installed most of the Carroll family heirlooms in the house.

The barrister and Mrs. Carroll's horticultural enthusiasm mandated innumerable orders to England for books, seeds, trees, grafts, roots, pots, and tools. Two indentured gardeners managed the acreage. An orangerie, erected circa 1760 in the barrister's bachelor years, was one of the first of its kind in Maryland. George Washington requested the dimensions of this so-called green house in 1784 in order to build one like it at Mount Vernon.

When the barrister died in 1783 at sixty years of age, he owned more than 33,000 acres in four counties and had a large interest in the Baltimore Iron Works. He was a primary lending source in lieu of banks before the Revolution and numbered wealthy men such as Edward Lloyd III and Charles Ridgely among his clients. The more than $7,000 he loaned Lafayette to supply his troops en route to Yorktown in 1781 was recounted to his heir with gratitude on Lafayette's 1824 return to America. Carroll is credited with helping draft Maryland's Constitution, serving as senator, and laying the foundation for Baltimore's industrial and mercantile future.

After Carroll's death, Margaret Tilghman Carroll lived at Mount Clare for thirty-four years as a widow. Her own income and an inheritance of half the barrister's estate per-

A craftsman named Kennedy from Ireland used Adam style fancy plastering when he remodeled the dining room mantel for Mrs. Carroll after her husband's death. Original Carroll furnishings in the dining room show the barrister's preference for "the neat, plain fassion and Calculated for lasting, nothing of the whimsical or Chinese taste which I abominate."

petuated Mount Clare's prosperity. Ensconced in a world of privilege made more social by Baltimore's having outstripped all Maryland cities in importance, "Peggy" Carroll made Mount Clare her primary residence. Circa 1789, she had the old-fashioned Georgian mantels in four rooms updated to the Federal style with applied plaster ornamentation, probably by the Irish plasterer James Kennedy, whose notice in the *Maryland Journal* advertised a specimen of his work at Mount Clare. She also had the bull's-eye window in the pediment of the garden façade altered to a more stylish lunette window. Tax records of 1798 reveal that Mount Clare was one of the most luxurious houses in Maryland.

At Margaret Carroll's death in 1817, Baltimore was a city of 8,000 and was encroaching on the genteel landscape of Mount Clare. James Maccubbin, who had inherited Mount Clare from his uncle, the barrister, with the provision that he change his name to Carroll, began relinquishing pieces of the estate to industrial development. Brick kilns proliferated, and the new B&O Railroad constructed Mount Clare

Station and the Carrollton Viaduct on the property. By the end of the third generation of Carroll ownership, the rented or leased Mount Clare was allotted progressively less and less upkeep until, by 1873, the wings and outbuildings had to be demolished.

A city beautification project in the late nineteenth century resulted in the purchase of 162 acres including Mount Clare and its gardens for a city park. New hyphens and wings were added to the main block in the spirit of Colonial Revivalism in 1908, but the restorative life force of Mount Clare did not arrive until 1917 when the National Society of the Colonial Dames of America in the State of Maryland opened the city property as a museum. Their assiduous research has located furnishings that match eighteenth-century orders made out by the barrister for objects in Europe. Today, original furnishings such as Margaret Carroll's suite of white and gilt Louis XV sofas and chairs (so different from her husband's inclination for pieces made in a plain fashion) shows how international colonial taste could be.

The 1985 restoration of the mansion's interior to its original paint colors marked the beginning stages of a plan that included reconstructing the original outbuildings and garden landscape. Only the house's main block and 113 acres of the original estate remain, but, happily, the core of the site with undisturbed foundations, undulating terraces, and orchard, vineyard, and garden locations is intact. State funding for the prodigious restoration in the southwest industrial section of Baltimore will elucidate the beauty and significance of the oldest building in Baltimore and first house museum in Maryland.

London Town Publik House

See-saw, sacaradown,
Which is the way to London town?
One foot up, the other down,
This is the way to London town.

Children of Olde England thought all roads led to London. The children of colonial Maryland knew better. Two Londons did, in fact, exist in the eighteenth-century English-speaking world. Both were trade centers, dispatching vessels to the four corners of the earth. Both were cynosures for the wealthy, famous, and ambitious men of the day. Yet one town endured while the other vanished.

Today, Maryland's ancient port of London Town survives in name only. One building within its former one-hundred-acre town limits is left. Not a street, not even an overgrown cellar hole can be seen. Only a solitary brick mansion surrounded by woods remains of a town that was an eighteenth-century crossroads of the world.

The London Town Publik House in Edgewater cuts a lonely figure on its knoll overlooking the South River. It is a relic from America's English past. Straightlaced in dignified Georgian proportions, it stands like a monument to a civilization which once teemed to its very door.

Over two hundred years ago, the house was an "ordinary," or inn, for travelers along the Eastern Seaboard. Fare of the day was served in the commodious hall. Food and spirits were also dispensed in the basement, primarily to the lower classes. Every room had a bed, and every bed could accommodate several occupants who were, more often than not, strangers to each other.

Judging from its size and architectural sophistication, the London Town Publik House must have been the finest ordinary in town, if not one of the finest in existence at the time. The all-header brick façade was an extravagant choice of brick bond and, except for several prestigious buildings in Annapolis, a rarity in America and England. The severe verticality of the two-story structure, broken by a molded brick water table at the elevated basement level and a belt course at the second-floor level, is softened by a wide, handsome cornice all around the roofline. A three-bay-wide central pavilion projects boldly from the seven-bay-wide south façade and is surmounted by a pediment with a single lunette window. The main entrance door is

OPPOSITE: *Accommodations in the basement were for servants of the planters who converged with their retinues on London Town at tobacco harvest time. London Town was one of a few Maryland ports designated by the British Crown to export tobacco.*

The Publik House displays its eighteenth-century function as an inn with an ordinary in the hall. Thomas Jefferson and George Washington refreshed themselves in the commodious hall while waiting for passage on the ferry that would take them three-quarters of a mile across the South River to a road that led to Annapolis.

located here and looks down on the once-bustling access road to the South River ferry. The whole structure speaks well of its builder's grasp of Georgian architectural tenets, and the two massive chimneys, harboring a deck at the abbreviated apex of the hipped roof, made a fine landmark for ships rounding Thomas Point from the Chesapeake Bay.

No account books survive, so we can only suppose that the elegant inn was well frequented. Certainly, the town swelled with each new harvest of Maryland tobacco. Planters, factors, servants, and slaves descended on London Town with great hogsheads of tobacco. The British tobacco fleet dropped anchor in the South River for six to nine months each year awaiting the inspection, sale, and loading of the tobacco. And local people, fortified with profits from the tobacco sales, bargained with the ships' captains for imported European and East Indian goods.

London Town was one of only a handful of Maryland ports designated by the Crown to export tobacco. Up until the town lost its port of entry status, the Publik House probably never suffered a dearth of guests. The thriving tobacco trade could fill every bed in the inn daily, and passengers waiting for the South River ferry over to Annapolis and points north probably commandeered every available seat in the hall and ordinary.

The South River ferry, docking at the foot of Scott Street, was part of the great north-south highway connecting Williamsburg and Philadelphia. Major roads in southern Maryland converged in London Town not only to accommodate the tobacco trade: Travelers intent on the shortest distance through the colonial wilderness eliminated many miles of a wearisome overland journey by taking the three-quarter-mile ferry ride across the South River. Gentry from Maryland and Virginia traveled to Annapolis in summer for the horse races, then again in winter for the social season. Statesmen and patriots made their way to and from Philadelphia. A complete passenger list from the South River ferry would serve as a directory for *Who's Who in Early American Society.*

William Brown, owner and operator of the ferry and the London Town Publik House, catered to Anne Arundel County's staunchest Loyalists. Anthony Stewart, forced by colonists to burn his tea-bearing brig, the *Peggy Stewart,* in 1775, retained a room once a year in the London Town Publik House. James Dick, another Loyalist and the man who owned most of London Town, including a sizable mortgage on Brown's Publik House, might have enjoyed the company of his friend Stewart in the privacy of the River Room.

Today, one can walk through the huge front door into the spacious entry passage and accurately imagine the welcome received by colonial wayfarers. Eighteenth-century inns were notoriously ill equipped, run-down, and vermin infested. But here was an establishment where even the cold drafts from the entry doors were ingeniously kept to a minimum: Directly off the entry passage, four corner rooms (located at the four corners of the building) were elevated six inches to block the flow of cold air under their doors.

In one of these rooms, a reproduction poster bed exhibits the usual equipage necessary for a good night's sleep two hundred years ago: Voluminous draperies, hanging from a canopy, kept out the cold air and evil humors of the

ABOVE: *Tea, set for the gentry in a corner room, recalls Anthony Stewart, whose tea-bearing brig* Peggy Stewart *was burned by patriots in 1775. He retained a room in the Publik House once a year.*

BELOW: *In the eighteenth century, a ferry operator was licensed by the county court and was expected to provide services to the public such as meals and lodging for ferry passengers. The owner of the London Town Publik House, William Brown, provided meals from this large basement kitchen.*

night; three mattresses—of corn husks, horse hair, and wool cardings, laid one atop the other—were comfortable but not inclined to stay put during the night; a large bolster beneath several pillows purportedly kept everything anchored, but by morning the gentleman who began his slumber comfortably sitting up might find himself hanging over the floor.

An unlikely source of information which has helped bring the London Town Publik House to life is a recent study of innkeeper Brown's mortgages. Those mortgages indicate that the construction of the eighteen-room structure took place not between 1744 and 1750 as was supposed, but between 1758 and 1764, and that it was a considerable, if not speculative, undertaking for Brown. Thirty years and three mortgages later, William Brown, unable to meet payments, lost the London Town Publik House.

Money matters probably plagued Brown before his inn was even completed. A comparison of the masterfully executed exterior with the plain, unembellished interior suggests that Brown could not finish the building in the style he originally intended.

The peculiarity of the unfinished interior is underscored by the fact that Brown was a cabinetmaker by trade. His connection with Mount Clare in Baltimore and the Upton Scott House in Annapolis emphasizes how important the trim work and moldings on mantels, doorways, and stairs would have been to him as an advertisement for his talents. And yet, where paneling would have traditionally hidden a bare brick fireplace, there is none. Nailing blocks embedded in the brick (for attaching the paneling) show not one nail hole. In the entire building, only the door of the River Room sports a decorative touch, and then its simple carving is lost in the overwhelming austerity of the rest of the interior.

Details aside, cabinetmaker-architect-ferrymaster-innkeeper Brown accomplished far more than he could have intended with his ambitious undertaking of the London Town Publik House. He built a singularly beautiful and enduring Georgian structure. When it outlived its usefulness as an inn in 1793, as a tenant house in the estate of Maryland Governor John Stone in 1806, and as a private house for James and Mary Larrimore circa 1828, the London Town Publik House became the Anne Arundel County Almshouse.

With its basic structure unaltered since 1758, including original glass and hardware, London Town Publik House is a superlative Georgian example of colonial architecture.

When the Welfare Act made the county home and its services obsolete in 1965, the house was reconditioned for use as a county museum. Its little-altered interiors with original cloak and hat boards, doors, hardware, and windows with original glass make it an unusually fine example of an eighteenth-century ordinary. The eleven acres surrounding the Publik House were landscaped and developed into an outstanding public arboretum and woodland garden. Twelve additional acres were annexed to the park in 1985 to provide a buffer from the modern-day community and to allow room for expansion. The Publik House was designated a National Historic Landmark in 1970 and was opened to the public in 1973.

Not a private house but an ordinary, the London Town Publik House is the only building that remains of a bustling eighteenth-century Maryland port. Its masonry construction used bricks placed head end out, an extravagant style indicative, perhaps, of the stature of its once-prominent environs.

In 1765, William Paca built the first five-part Georgian mansion in Annapolis. It was the first house of its kind in a city described half a century earlier as ". . . situate on a Plain, Where scarce a house will keep out Rain."[1] Three stories high, with thirty-seven rooms, and set, formidably, on an embankment several feet above the street level, its distinctive design, based on the theories of the sixteenth-century architect Palladio, was the vogue in England, and its two-acre garden was described by a contemporary traveler as the most elegant in Annapolis.

In 1965, the site was slated for demolition. The massive brick mansion had been engulfed during the twentieth century by the superstructure of Carvel Hall, a 200-room hotel. Its fabulous garden had been obliterated by a landfill, a parking lot, and a bus station. In two hundred years, Paca's house and garden had sunk to its nadir—the planned replacement would be a modern high-rise.

There is a lesson for the world and for posterity in the prompt and effective action taken by the citizens of Annapolis to save the Paca House and Garden. Historic Annapolis, Inc., a small, almost impoverished preservationist group, not only rescued the site from demolition and delivered the National Historic Landmark District from a proposed eyesore; its members also raised the money to restore the Paca House, developed a long-term plan for its self-sufficiency, and persuaded the State of Maryland to purchase and rejuvenate the garden.

The reward for their eight-year struggle must ultimately be the appearance today of the restored landmark. But fate has bestowed a bonus on their efforts, one which has reaped national accolades. Beneath two centuries and untold tons of rubble behind the Paca House, archeologists unearthed the extensive remains of Paca's *original* garden, including five spacious terraces, traces of a pond, and the foundations of several garden structures. Instead of a mere facsimile of an eighteenth-century garden, the State of Maryland was now able to restore what appeared to be one of the finest gardens in colonial America.

Such a major archeological find is rare, but everything about Historic Annapolis's meticulous research in the building's restoration and the State of Maryland's thorough garden restoration has been uncommon. X rays beamed through wooden staircases in the derelict Carvel Hall Hotel offered proof that the building contained features pre-

Paca House

OPPOSITE: *William Paca's eighteenth-century garden behind his Annapolis town house was reconstructed from archeological evidence of the original walls and wilderness lake found under nine feet of rubble and a 200-room hotel. So prized was the colonial garden by Paca that he had Charles Willson Peale feature it as a backdrop in his formal portrait.*

served from Paca's own day. An electron microscope was used to analyze as many as twenty layers of paint in the house to determine the original colors on Mr. Paca's walls. The subsequent discovery of a brilliant peacock blue on the first-floor walls has revolutionized the standard palette associated with colonial interiors. The restoration of that distinctive Prussian blue, labeled "Paca House blue," to the first-floor walls of the house after 1975 was regarded as appalling by authorities at other historic mansions but has since been accepted as accurate for the pre-Revolutionary War period. Similarly brilliant wall color has now been introduced in Mount Vernon, house interiors at Williamsburg, and exhibits in the American Wing of the Metropolitan Museum of Art.

Extensive archival research turned up the source for the eighteenth-century design for the exquisitely carved mantel in the parlor. A picture in a 1741 edition of a British builder's handbook duplicates the mantel in every way save one: the oak leaves in the frieze are an American species, not British.

Two hundred pieces of William Paca's prodigious set of Nanking china turned up at a 1905 estate sale on the Eastern Shore. The covers of the vegetable dishes were missing, and eventually they arrived, too, via a Paca descendant in Arizona who happened to ask if the house had any use for Nanking china vegetable dish covers!

The hoopla over such seemingly trivial discoveries is entirely justified. Paca House researchers were faced with bleak prospects at the outset of their task to bring to life the history of the Paca House. All traces of Paca and his family had been erased from the building. A dearth of information relating to the Annapolis lifestyle of this formidable lawyer, patriot, and governor of Maryland stymied archival sleuths at every turn. It is known that William Paca jealously guarded his privacy and preferred to work less ostentatiously in the service of his country than did his fellow patriots.

Even the pronunciation of Paca's name has presented some mystery. Witness the contrasting pronunciations of Paca Street (Pack-ah) in Baltimore and Paca House (Pay-ka) in Annapolis. A rhyming couplet, presumably written by Paca, from the 1771 notes of the Annapolis Hominy Club, conclusively establishes how his name was spoken by his contemporaries:

The best room in Mr. Paca's house was very different from the stark simplicity of the rest of the house. He remodeled his parlor some ten years after the house was built, incorporating a filigree of neoclassical plaster ornamentation around the overmantel. The crimson-colored moreen reefed curtains duplicate a popular period color.

And so do I, tho' cannot but think we take a rash step in so doing, but no more than Will Paca.[2]

Will Paca's reclusive lifestyle limits the extent to which one might link the man and his home. The broader interpretation, however, reveals how a prominent eighteenth-century Annapolitan might have used his house and garden. The historical insights are multi-leveled.

First, the building is impressive, as much today as it was

when it was built in 1765. Three different styles of brick bonding are incorporated into its five-bay center section; the all-header bond of the front façade helped establish that distinctive style in Annapolis. A belt course of Flemish bond brickwork with glazed headers ornaments the front façade as do a simple box cornice and splayed, gauged-brick, flat arches over the door and window openings. The steep gable roof with the interior end chimneys displays five dormers on the front and two on the back, their size, shape, and even existence based on an early dormer discovered in one of the initial architectural investigations of the hotel. A generous stone foundation, its crevices laced with a pretty pattern of small stones called galleting, enhances the building's big, solid mass. The center section is connected by one-story hyphens to the perpendicularly placed one-story dependencies. The size of this house would be overwhelming were its parts not perfectly balanced, in consummate harmony with the tenets of Georgian architecture.

Twenty-three-year-old William Paca, lately graduated as a Master of Arts from the College of Philadelphia and an aspiring lawyer in Annapolis's most prestigious law firm, could afford the grandiose undertaking. In 1763, he married an amiable young lady with a considerable fortune.

Molly Chew Paca's ample resources allowed the young couple to purchase two sizable city lots four days after their wedding and to build on the site a house that would take two years to finish and that would set a standard for architectural excellence in the colonial capital. They probably moved into their town house well before the interior was completed.

To some eyes, the interior may still appear incomplete. Behind the mammoth front door (which well accommodated Paca's six-foot frame), a wide and lofty passage of almost severe simplicity extends the width of the house. Its bare, unvarnished floor of rough pine planking is without carpets. The brilliant Prussian blue sets off the plainly molded woodwork, and a few fine side chairs line the wall. The starkness is accurate. In fact, British museum experts are thrilled with the rusticity of the sand-scrubbed floors and the colorful walls, for they are authentic to period houses in England.

Just off the passage is a room more in keeping with the sumptuous interiors Americans have grown to expect of

Paca House blue adorns the trim of a room set up for dining. Painted floor cloths, this one parqueted and marbleized for a grand effect, saved wear on floors and were easily replaced. The portrait is of Anna Maria Chew, Paca's sister-in-law.

colonial America's Georgian period. The parlor is a room that architectural historians surmise was redesigned by the Pacas some five to ten years after the house was built to keep up with the avant-garde Adam influence being worked into Hammond's and Lloyd's new houses down the street. Too, William Paca's prominence in the cause for liberty probably brought the most important people in the colonies to this parlor. In their league, a stylish parlor was de rigueur.

X rays through the wood of the staircase banisters revealed that both styles were original to the eighteenth century. The turned banisters were considered more formal than the fanciful Chinese Chippendale motif on the second floor.

Several archaic architectural features contribute to the internal layout. The hall, an unpretentious room across from the parlor, is a holdover from medieval England. It was used then as a gathering place, and, in Paca's day, as an informal parlor. The porch, a two-story tower joined to the back of the house, is an Elizabethan period feature rarely found in early American architecture. From the outside, its slender proportions give the house a distinctive Old English appearance. Possibly, Paca himself incorporated the plan of the porch into the plan of his house, for the view from its three second-story windows is of his beloved garden.

Historians know that Paca's two-acre stretch of undulating terraces, with its wilderness pond and distant view of the Severn River, was important to him. He had Charles Willson Peale paint his portrait with the garden as a backdrop instead of a more formal setting indicative of his station in life. In the twentieth century, the portrait's background showing several garden structures enabled architects to recreate the garden pavilion and the Chinese trellis-pattern bridge exactly as they appeared in Paca's day.

As lovely as Paca's garden was to contemplate, beauty was not its sole function in the colonial scheme of things. A close look at the meticulously interlaced plantings reveals an abundance of useful culinary and medicinal herbs. The shady arbor is hung with gourds, convertible to dippers; the pond is fringed with rushes for scouring pots; and some garden walls have espaliered fruit trees. Self-sufficiency in the eighteenth century was as vital to the city dweller as it was to the plantation master. In Paca's garden, however, we are taken a step further and discover how mutually complementary beauty and practicality can be.

The same spirit of ingenuity continues to the present day. A conservation program, in the Middendorf Conservation Center, propagates Maryland's endangered botanical species and makes them available to private gardeners. Paca's house combines museum programs with thoroughly modern facilities for conferences and meetings. Its third floor contains well-equipped bedrooms for visiting guests of the state and federal governments. Even the impeccable furnishings of Paca's second-floor period rooms don twentieth-century trimmings when the house becomes a temporary home for global luminaries.

Perhaps it is no accident that Paca's house and garden have survived several centuries despite overwhelming odds to the contrary. There is a strength of will and flexibility about the place that has allowed it to adapt to the demands of the changing times.

In order to use the Paca House as a guesthouse for distinguished guests of the state and federal governments, second-floor rooms feature fine, durable furnishings such as the mideighteenth-century mahogany tall post bed with cabriole legs and a circa 1725 William and Mary blanket chest with bun feet.

Brice House

There is a two-foot-square block of sandstone in the southwest corner of the Brice House cellar that is crudely incised with the words "The Beginning." The inscription identifies the cornerstone laid in 1767.

In an account book James Brice kept for itemizing the cost of building his house, only one precisely quilled entry refers to the cornerstone: "Rum at laying Corner Stone"[1] on April 14, 1767.

Understatement characterizes contemporary references to the house Brice built in Annapolis. Understatement, however, does not jibe with the monumentality of this structure that was seven years in the making and one of the largest private houses built in colonial America.

Set regally on a terrace above quaint, quiet East Street, the Brice House dominates all but its near neighbor, the Paca House. Bereft of most of the original grounds, once as deep and as wide on the north as the Paca Gardens, the Brice House seems outsized on its lot, and its formal Georgian architecture does not dispel that impression.

Five parts—a central block of all header bricks flanked by two hyphens and two wings after Palladio's popular design—extend 156 feet along the street. Boosted by an elevated cellar of Susquehanna stone, the two-and-a-half-story height of the central block is emphasized by a steeply pitched roof and enormous end chimneys soaring sixty feet above the ground. Windows that are proportionally small in the five-bay-wide north and south façades exaggerate the building's magnitude. The long one-and-a-half-story hyphens and wings serve handsomely, however, to balance the otherwise severe verticality and bulk of the structure.

Hyperbole suits the Brice House much more than understatement. Exaggeration in a manner at once grand and severe is its forté. In the twentieth century its panache was recognized: one of the first efforts to restore colonial Annapolis was initiated with the purchase of the Brice House in the early part of the century. The Security Land Company of New Jersey's plan to establish an Institute of American Studies failed (Brice House was subsequently subdivided by St. John's College for faculty apartments), but the scheme at least established and safeguarded the building's importance. By contrast, extant records of the Brice House at the time it was built don't reveal a particular significance to the growing colonial capital. We can only infer how An-

napolis was affected by a house with construction costs that amounted to a princely £4,014 8s upon completion.

Of course, the Paca House nearby had already set a lavish standard for the city in 1765, and Governor Horatio Sharpe's Whitehall, outside Annapolis, had just the year before scaled the heights of British architectural fashion in the colonies. But Brice House, coming fast on their heels, was one the big, early town houses in the colonial development of Annapolis that later would produce the Chase-Lloyd, Hammond-Harwood, Upton Scott, and Ridout houses. Just maybe the port's growth made a quantum leap when a family of wealth and position like the Brices invested so confidently in its future.

A gargantuan pile that majestically engulfs its present-day lot in Annapolis is the town house James Brice built between 1767 and 1773. The 1971 discovery in a vault in Baltimore of Colonel Brice's eighteenth-century book accounting for every aspect of the construction makes the house one of the best-documented historic buildings in Maryland.

Carving still crisp after more than two centuries pays tribute to the artisans who labored over it. William Bampton received £40 for "finishing the largest room in My House," noted James Brice in his account book. A shallow carving style juxtaposed to a deeper, more flamboyant execution indicates, however, that two artisans may have worked on the ornate mantel.

John Brice, the first of that name in America, immigrated to Annapolis from London around 1696 to serve as agent for the London merchants Benjamin Hatley & Company. He operated their store and warehouse of consigned English goods and West Indian merchandise in a building that architectural historians maintain was the west wing of the Brice House. His ownership of lands along the Severn River included the plantation Pendennis Mount and qualified him as a man of stature in the colonies; he was elected to the Lower House of the Maryland General Assembly.

The success of his son, John Brice II, lay in his profession as an attorney, his position as judge of the Provincial Court, and his marriage to Sarah Frisby, great-granddaughter of land baron Augustine Hermann of Bohemia Manor. Judge Brice's landholdings extended to counties on the Eastern Shore, but he maintained a legal office and residence in the brick, gambrel-roofed dwelling on Prince George Street known as the "little Brice House." Lot 94 in Annapolis, which the judge inherited from his father, was obliquely across the street from the little Brice House. According to the judge's will of 1766, the lot was being developed with lot 103 (providing contiguous land to the north) for a dwelling house.

The judge's second son, James (or "Jemmie," as he was referred to in family letters), inherited the two lots as stipulated at his father's death in 1766:

> To James Brice . . . my Lott of Land in the City of Annapolis . . . by Stoddert's resurvey of said City is numbered 94 & also a lott of Land . . . numbered by said resurvey 103 also all the Bricks Lime and Stone Plank & Timber already worked up or to be worked up & which I have made Burnt & raised for the purpose of Building a dwelling House & out Houses on one of the Lotts.[2]

The judge's eldest son, John, it should be noted, also received a share of his father's estate, but as the scion of one of the wealthiest of Maryland's planter aristocrats, he had been packed off to England several years earlier to be educated. An English education for the second son was discussed upon Judge Brice's death but was never fulfilled, and James, age twenty in 1766, remained at home amidst the privileges and pleasures of his class.

The account book James Brice kept over many years of

Vibrant blue was the original color of the largest room in the Brice House. Seven elaborate plaster moldings in the cornice and an abundance of fine wood carving on the fireplace indicate that the room was, possibly, a parlor for entertainment.

his life notes extravagant early expenditures, undoubtedly associated with his membership in the new Governor Eden's select coterie of friends. Subscriptions to balls, theater tickets, silk hose and silver buckles, dinner at the Fox Hunter's Club, gaming, and the horse races were not, however, indicative of a rake's progress. One year after his father's death, twenty-one-year-old James was building the house his father seemed at least to have gathered materials for. The project, funded by revenues from James's newly inherited plantations in Cecil County and his mother's cash infusions, was accounted for down to the smallest expenditure for nails under the heading "Cost of Erecting Buildings on Lots in Annapolis Nos. 94 and 103 Begun 1767 by Ja. Brice."[3]

Today, James Brice's account book—miraculously dis-

Colonel James Brice, who was interim Governor of Maryland in 1792 and a member of the wealthy land-owning class, incorporated the finest craftsmanship of the period in his town abode, the construction of which he personally oversaw. The windows have hand-carved sashes and paneled shutters that retract into the walls when not in use.

covered in a vault of the Masonic Temple on Charles Street in Baltimore in 1971—is fabulously important not only as primary documentation for the construction of so important a colonial house but also as illustration of the full extent of young Brice's direction, apparently without the services of an architect or builder. Any stylistic links the house may have previously seemed to have with colonial architect William Buckland, for example, are now questionable because nowhere in Brice's meticulous accounting does he record payment to Buckland or, for that matter, any architect/master builder.

Many colonial gentlemen developed their own architectural plans based on pattern books published in England. They directed the workmen themselves in much the same way an enterprising twentieth-century individual will serve as his own general contractor, hiring subcontractors for various stages of construction. The masons, bricklayers, joiners, and carpenters Brice paid, and the tools he purchased for them suggest a major investment of his time, talent, money, and interest in the years between 1767 and 1773.

The product of his investment was provincial in many ways and not as sophisticated as the Paca, Hammond-Harwood, and Chase-Lloyd houses. Some of the delicate classical details on the exterior, specifically the second-story Palladian type window and unusual arch motif in the cornice, are lost in the building's massive, almost arrogant proportions. More successful are the proportions and ornamentation on the interior. Orlando Ridout IV suggests in his thesis on the James Brice House that the pleasant room arrangement may have come from the little Brice House that James Brice would have grown up in across the street.[4] A small, winding "secret" staircase in that older house seems comfortably copied in the gentlemen's parlor of the Brice House.

Fourteen rooms, not including halls, closets, attic rooms, and a wine cellar, compose the big house's asymmetrical floor plan. The east wing housed a kitchen, laundry, and servants' quarters, while the west wing probably accommodated a store and later a coach house. In his account book, James Brice never designated the use for his rooms. He made references to the dining room and parlor but we do not know which was which. He could have used the small room beside the entry hall in the main house as an

The room where Washington and Lafayette may have dined with Colonel Brice features unusual raised plaster paneling and wainscoting molded when it was wet to look like sections of wood. The raised paneling was painted yellow and glazed to duplicate the room's original color.

office. The inventory of James Brice's worldly goods made at his death lists a large number of Philadelphia Windsor chairs in the passage outside this office.

The great mahogany staircase in the entry hall with carved C-scroll stair ends and a molded handrail is the first indication of the interior's finesse. Beyond it, a parlor (sometimes referred to as the ballroom), painted a lively, original turquoise (decreed by twentieth-century electron microscope paint analysis), is the most spectacular room in the house, with its elaborate cornice, said to be more detailed than any in Annapolis, and its carved wood mantelpiece emblazoned with rococo motifs of the eighteenth-

century joiner's art. Two styles of carving on the fireplace seem evident to architectural historians Charles Phillips and Paul Buchanan, who studied Brice House[5] in the 1980s. Possibly James Brice paid two men to carve the fabulous fireplace. One of them, William Bampton, recorded in Brice's account book as having carved the chimneypiece in the largest room of the house, fled town, according to county court records, when he couldn't repay a debt.

The room designated the dining room by James Brice probably contained two mahogany dining tables and a dozen chairs that he purchased in Philadelphia in 1771. Raised plaster paneling adorns the glazed, ocher-colored, mahogany-grained walls. This later Adamesque style reflects how design trends changed in the house over its seven-year-long construction.

The green room, or gentlemen's parlor, may be the place where, according to local legend, James Brice entertained prestigious friends like George Washington and the Marquis de Lafayette. Brice's career included a commission as a colonel of the Maryland Militia, membership on the Governor's Council, and, after the Revolution, twice mayor of Annapolis and interim governor of Maryland in 1792. He was married in 1781 at the age of thirty-four to seventeen-year-old Juliana Jenings, and fathered five children in the big town house in Annapolis.

When James Brice died in 1801, his widow inherited the house and lived there with two of her sons until her death. A ghost story associated with the house concerns the death, purportedly at the hands of a manservant, of one of these sons. Late one night, the eighty-year-old man was hit on the head with a heavy object. He died shortly afterward, and his ghost was later "heard" in the halls of Brice House. In 1876, James Brice's grandchildren sold the property out of the family, and in 1970, thanks to the capable and generous ministrations of its last private owners, Mr. and Mrs. Stanley Wohl, the house was designated a National Historic Landmark.

Sold at auction to settle the Wohls' estate in 1982 to the International Union of Bricklayers and Allied Craftsmen, the house is being rehabilitated and adapted as headquarters for the $13 billion masonry industry in the United States and Canada. The International Masonry Institute takes special pride in the work of the eighteenth-century craftsmen who built Brice House. They consider the build-

ing a monument to the bricklayer's and plasterer's art in North America. The Maryland Historical Trust has an easement on the entire exterior so that it can never be altered. Historic Annapolis, Inc.'s, easement on the first floor of the main block permits that organization to show those rooms to the public for one hundred days a year. The rooms are being restored to the period of the building's 1767–1774 construction. The wings and hyphens, adapted for modern use, furnish research, conference, and training facilities for the International Masonry Institute.

Brice House was a showplace for several hundred years and at the last a still-viable vessel for the mystique and hauteur of Annapolis in its golden age. Under the aegis of its present owners, who are dedicated to its uniqueness and have been aided by the discovery of the original account book of construction, Brice House promises new perspectives on eighteenth-century architecture.

LEFT: *Stair ends on the main staircase are carved with a flourish of acanthus leaves and bordered by a continuous line of fretwork. Brice paid a man named Robert Key for finding the mahogany and making a handrail and banisters of it for his house.*

RIGHT: *Although maintained by the International Masonry Institute as an architectural monument and conference center for its industry's use, Brice House is not without moody vestiges of the past. The last Brice to live in the house gave it a ghostly reputation after he died there violently in the nineteenth century.*

Chase-Lloyd House

The three-story Chase-Lloyd House stands above its contemporaries in the heart of colonial Annapolis. So, too, did its earliest owners, Judge Samuel Chase, signer of the Declaration of Independence, and Edward Lloyd IV, dubbed "the magnificent" for his stupendous wealth and lavish lifestyle. In stature, in design, in its connection with these prominent Maryland patriots, the Chase-Lloyd House is an enduring testament to the grandeur of youthful Annapolis.

During its early years, the mansion hosted America's most brilliant society. Dinner parties during the gala winter season commingled statesmen, European guests, and Maryland gentry. Romance flourished behind its stately mien not once, but five times, as the Lloyd daughters fell in love and were married in their city home. The nuptials of the youngest daughter occurred in January 1802 in the first-floor hall: lovely Mary Tayloe Lloyd became the wife of twenty-two-year-old St. John's graduate Francis Scott Key.

The history of the Chase-Lloyd House began many years before, in 1769. The setting, Annapolis, was a city of consummmate elegance, acclaimed by one European visitor as "repleat with luxury, as sophisticated as Paris, and the sole center of what little art there is in America." If Annapolis encouraged a reputation for splendid living, it also promoted free thinking. Amidst the wealth, the wit, and the learning grew the seeds of rebellion. The move to break with Lord Baltimore's proprietary government was strong in colonial Annapolis, and in the vanguard of the movement was Samuel Chase. Depending upon their political allegiances, Maryland bigwigs considered Chase either a rabble-rouser or an inspired patriot. The florid, six-foot Chase was indeed fiercely ambitious and vehemently opposed to British rule. As a lawyer and member of Maryland's General Assembly, he found that permanent residence in Annapolis was necessary to the furtherance of his career. In 1769, at the age of twenty-eight, Samuel Chase purchased Lot No. 107, one block from State Circle, in the center of the city's finest residential district. He paid Denton Hammond £100 for the parcel, imported an artisan named Scott from England to oversee construction, and immediately began laying the foundation for a magnificent town house.

The enormity of Chase's architectural undertaking was exceeded only by his ambition. Son of a landless Somerset County clergyman, Sam Chase intended to build one of the

OPPOSITE: *The great cantilevered staircase in the center hall of the Chase-Lloyd House in Annapolis was a feat of construction in 1774 and remains a thing of unrivaled beauty for the symmetry and framing of its classical elements. The man who financed the completion of the house after its builder almost went bankrupt was dubbed "the magnificent" by his friends. His daughter married Francis Scott Key in the hall.*

The large, dramatic Palladian window lighting the wide stair landing is centered on the exterior of the rear façade. The graceful window overlooked the Lloyds' eighteenth-century gardens and a ten-foot-high wall separating the Lloyds' and Ogles' town properties.

OPPOSITE, ABOVE: *The delicate tracery of plasterwork on the second-floor hall ceiling anticipated America's infatuation with the neoclassical work of Robert Adam, then in vogue in London. Lloyd's town house with William Buckland in charge was in the vanguard of colonial interior design.*
OPPOSITE, BELOW: *William Buckland's motifs in his orchestration of the rich interiors mimicked ropes, ribbons, roses, leaves, and architectural elements. Tiny dogwood flowers frame the panels of the dining room's solid mahogany doors.*

finest houses Annapolis had ever seen, second only to that of Charles Carroll of Carrollton, the wealthiest man in the colonies. However, two years after the initial land purchase, Chase sold the unfinished house, and Carroll, with gentlemanly aplomb, hinted that a dearth of funds had forced the sale. " . . . It is however agreed on all hands that Chase has acted very wisely in selling it: he has got rid of an encumbrance which must have ruined him at ye long run: the money received of Lloyd will extricate him from all difficulties; he is now independent, and may if he pleases continue so and become more serviceable to the Public."[1] Happily, Chase went on to great public service, eventually attaining an appointment to the Supreme Court through President Washington.

His unfinished house found a buyer immediately, and while Chase, himself, would never enjoy the palatial town house, his dream for it would be realized in the extravagant plans of the second owner. In July 1771, for a price of £504.8.2 sterling plus £2,491.17.7 Maryland currency, Edward Lloyd IV became the owner of the property including "all houses, edifices, buildings, improvements, waters, easements, privileges, commodities and advantages whatsoever."[2]

Lloyd knew none of the financial restrictions that beset Chase. The Lloyd family, since arriving in Maryland in 1650, had accumulated several fortunes, hundreds of thousands of Eastern Shore acres, and four times as many slaves as the next ranking landowner. So fabulous was the Lloyd fortune that Richard Bennett Lloyd, Edward's younger brother, was able to win the hand of London's most celebrated beauty of the day. Edward himself enjoyed a life more akin to British nobility than Maryland gentry; his stable of horses was among the best in America, and his schooner was a legend in its own time. Awnings, rugs, pillows, and pennants adorned the vessel, and a brass cannon announced its arrival in Annapolis harbor. Shorter journeys required the use of a ten-oared barge manned by slaves dressed in azure and gold livery.

Edward Lloyd IV was twenty-seven years old when he bought the Chase mansion. He was tall, handsome, and already accustomed to the best life had to offer. The birth of a first child and the triumph of his first election to the Maryland General Assembly inspired the purchase, but judging from the condition of the Chase mansion at the time of the sale, Lloyd would require more than a little time and money to bring the residence up to Lloyd family standards.

The mansion was unfinished. The three-story structure on its high foundation measured fifty-four feet wide by forty-three feet deep. The salmon-colored brick walls were laid in Flemish bond and ornamented by belt courses of rubbed brick at the second- and third-floor levels. A cornice enriched the roofline, and a central pavilion of three bays crowned with a pediment and bull's-eye window projected from the seven-bay front façade. Walls were eighteen inches thick, and flooring had been laid, but the interior was barren, and a roof was still in the offing.

Edward Lloyd wasted no time in hiring the most fashionable architect in Annapolis to prepare the house for decidedly elegant habitation. An entry in Lloyd's business ledgers records payment to the renowned William Buckland, £3 "for the expense of [him]Self and Horse when I purchased New House."[3] From 1771 until 1772, Lloyd's ledgers show that architect, designer, and carver Buckland was in complete charge of the city house. The designs for the highly ornate plaster ceilings in the parlor and dining room, executed by the British craftsmen Barnes and Rallins, are thought to be examples of Buckland's amazingly rich work in the Chase-Lloyd House. (Unfortunately, the dining room plaster ceiling fell victim to plumbing problems in the 1960s.) The more delicate tracery of the ceiling plasterwork in the hall and second floor herald, with true Buckland prescience, the popularity of the post-Revolutionary War Adam style. The basic plan of the house—four rooms with a center hall—deviates from that norm with the inclusion of lateral halls between the front and rear rooms and with the monumental proportions of the first-floor rooms. The sixteen-by-forty-foot center hall was large enough to accommodate receptions, balls, and, most ideally, the weddings of the Lloyd daughters. Two freestanding Ionic columns frame a cantilevered staircase which was a construction tour de force in 1774. A large and extraordinarily graceful Palladian window lights the magnificent stairs and most of the long, handsome hall.

From 1772 until completion in 1774, Buckland, heavily committed to other clients, was supplanted by William Noke. Although Buckland and Noke shared in overseeing the completion of the house, the elaborate and highly

The Chase-Lloyd House, the only three-story house in Annapolis, was also one of the first of its height erected in the colonies. A legendary agreement between its owner and the owner of the Hammond-Harwood House directly across the street purportedly guaranteed an unobscured view of Annapolis harbor from the third-story windows.

imaginative interior detail is generally attributed to Buckland. In spite of three different architects, the character of the house emerges as an integrated whole, considered by historians to be one of the earliest and finest examples of the Adam influence in America.

One approaches the Chase-Lloyd House from Maryland Avenue. As in colonial days, a white paling borders the property and curves gracefully to meet the wide entrance stair. A berm or embankment behind the white fence runs parallel to the house on the south side to shield the backyard from the street. Its eighteenth-century construction, obviously for privacy, brings to mind the legendary agreement between Mr. Lloyd and Mr. Hammond, whose house is across the street. Did Mathias Hammond agree to limit the height of his fine Palladian mansion so that Edward Lloyd could have some view of the Chesapeake from his third-floor rooms? No one knows for sure. The Chase-Lloyd House is, however, one of the first full three-story brick Georgian town houses to be erected in the colonies, and it has been acclaimed the finest ever built in the southern colonies.

In 1846, the mansion was sold out of the Lloyd family to a Chase family, cousins of the first owner. In an appropriate

OPPOSITE: The doors of the dining room are solid mahogany fitted with original bell silver drop pulls and escutcheons and framed by carved rope moldings possibly of architect William Buckland's design. Buckland, the architect most in demand in Annapolis, is documented to have worked on finishing the interiors of the Chase-Lloyd House.

The fabulous ornate ceiling plasterwork executed by English artisans characterized Edward Lloyd's ostentatious lifestyle in Annapolis. No expense was spared for the town residence of one of the richest men in the province. The house is now a home for aged and infirm gentlewomen run by a board of directors for the Maryland Diocese of the Protestant Episcopal Church.

A preponderance of paling painted gleaming white distinguishes the formal entrance to the big pre-Revolutionary War town house. A brass knocker on the front door in the shape of the head of a little girl was brought by Edward Lloyd IV from his Eastern Shore plantation and recalls the five Lloyd daughters who grew up and were married in the Annapolis house.

twist of fate, ownership then descended to the grandchildren of Sam Chase. One might happily end the story here, the mansion miraculously restored to the progeny of its first owner. But history revealed one more quirk in the ensuing drama of Chase-Lloyd ownership. In 1886, Hester Ann Chase Ridout, granddaughter of Sam Chase, willed the house to a board of trustees with membership in the Protestant Episcopal Church as a home for aged gentlewomen. In so doing, she completed a family saga that began over one hundred years earlier with the son of a landless, penniless Anglican clergyman. In its final owner, the Chase-Lloyd House—registered as a National Historic Landmark in 1965—seems assured of preservation and establishes a memorial to its creators, Samuel Chase and Edward Lloyd IV.

So grand are the five-part Palladian mansions of the eighteenth century that first impressions obscure one of the most important functions of their size—accommodation. Wealthy planters required large quarters not only for their families and servants, but also for relations and friends, who often visited for months at a time. The largesse that characterized the hospitality of these planters made their stylish houses beacons of comfort in a countryside woefully short on inns and long on distances.

Montpelier's hospitality is well documented. George Washington's diaries record overnight stays at this Prince George's County mansion on his trips to and from the Constitutional Conventional of 1787. Martha Washington and her retinue spent a wet spring night in 1789 on their way to her husband's inauguration in New York. They were urged by Montpelier's hostess to make the house a stop whenever they traveled the nearby Post Road between George Town and Baltimore. Most revealing of all the accounts by distinguished visitors taking shelter for a night was that of a New Englander unaccustomed to imposing herself on private houses. Wrote Abigail Adams en route to John Adams's presidential inauguration in 1800:

> Last winter there was a Gentleman and Lady in Philadelphia by the name of Snowden whose hospitality I heard much of . . . I was advised at Baltimore to make their House my stage for the night . . . but I who have never been accustomed to quarter myself and servants upon private houses, could not think of it, particularly as I [had with me] ten Horses and nine persons. I therefore ordered the coachman to proceed [past their house]. We had got about a mile when we were stoped by the Major in full speed, who had learnt I was comeing on; and had kept watch for me, with his Horse at the door . . . In the kindest, and politest manner he urged my return to his House, represented the danger of the road, and the impossibility of my being accomodated at any Inn I could reach: A mere hovel was all I should find. I plead my numbers. That was no objection. He could accomodate double that number. There was no saying nay and I returnd to a large, Handsome, Elegant House where I was received with my Family, with what we might term true English Hospitality . . .[1]

Montpelier

Emmanuel Havenith, Belgium's minister plenipotentiary, renovated a wing and added a bell to Montpelier's gable when he owned the house in 1916.

Architectural historians date Montpelier's construction to 1770–1785, roughly contemporaneous with the firebacks in the fireplaces of several bedrooms. The cast iron slabs, traditionally used to protect the rear bricks and radiate heat into the rooms, are simply ornamented with raised printing,

S
T A
1783

for Major Thomas Snowden and his wife Ann Ridgely Snowden. Major Snowden, whose personal seal was a heart inscribed with his initials, confided to George Washington's nephew, Robert Lewis, in 1789, that his wife, Ann Ridgely, was "an heiress to an immense estate and married him merely for love."[2] Romantic inclination might also have prompted the Snowdens to commemorate the first occupancy of their house with initialed, dated firebacks made at the family's Patuxent Iron Works.

Montpelier's design was not unusual for a family of means in America in the second half of the eighteenth century. Georgian elegance characterized its five-part Palladian system. Quality materials and workmanship were lavished on its English and Flemish bond brickmasonry. Located far from any habitation decades before Snowden's son, Nicholas, would establish the village of Laurel, its hilltop environs, postmarked the intersection of the Patuxent River and the Great Northern and Southern Post Road, were nonetheless assiduously contoured. They were garnished with the kind of summerhouse Europeans called a belvedere, for the beautiful views framed by its small windows.

Montpelier's center block of two stories plus an attic was built first. Later, though how much later is uncertain, single-story hyphens connected the center block to handsome, rectangular, two-story wings with semi-octagonal ends. James T. Wollon, Jr., contended in his 1979 architectural study of Montpelier that Plate 26 of William Halfpenny's *A New and Complete System of Architecture,* 1749, a book available in early America, may have been the source of Montpelier's design.[3] William Buckland was once thought to have had some influence on Montpelier's design: his work on the Hammond-Harwood House exhibits marked similarity to Montpelier's wings with semi-octagonal ends and

The rear façade of Montpelier is as grand as the front. The projecting pavilion of the center block is reminiscent of William Buckland's design for the Hammond-Harwood House in Annapolis.

A beacon of comfort on the long Post Road that stretched between Virginia and New England in the eighteenth century, Montpelier has a history of accommodating wayfarers. Abigail Adams, much impressed by its owners' largesse, described Montpelier as "a large, Handsome, Elegant House."

Did George Washington sleep in this handsomely paneled first-floor room? In May and September of 1787 he lodged at Major Snowden's, but the exact room is a mystery.

also to the center block's projecting pavilion surmounted by a pediment with a bull's-eye window. No documentation has yet come to light, however, linking William Buckland with Montpelier.

When Thomas Snowden began building Montpelier, much of the surrounding countryside belonged to his family. Four generations of Snowdens preceded him in Maryland, each accruing more land than the last in what was then Charles and Calvert counties. Richard Snowden, a Welsh-born Quaker, settled in the province of Maryland in 1658. His grandson, also Richard Snowden, was the iron master who built the Patuxent Iron Works and bequeathed three sons more than 12,260 acres of land in southern Maryland in 1763.

Thomas Snowden, Richard the iron master's grandson, born in 1751, was nineteen years old when he began accumulating chunks of family property. Four hundred acres of his father's property plus a significant share in the iron works were his upon his father's death in 1770. Another portion of the family property went to Thomas when a brother died in 1775 and bequeathed him his inheritance.

In 1774 at the age of twenty-five, Thomas Snowden married Ann Ridgely, daughter of Colonel Henry and Ann Dorsey Ridgely of Anne Arundel County. Legend attributes more extravagance to the celebration of their nuptials than Quaker sensibility was comfortable with: young Snowden was barred from Quaker meeting. Only after he purportedly freed some of his slaves was he welcomed back into the fold.

In 1776, Thomas Snowden was commissioned initially a second major of the 25th Battalion of Militia of Prince George's County and then a first major of the Upper Battalion of Militia of Prince George's County. His "major" status stuck with him long after the Revolutionary War. His association with George Washington was also long-lived, bringing to the family iron works the general's highly complimentary orders for ploughs and shears. Although Snowden preferred to credit his wife as the source of family status and wealth, describing himself as "of obscure parentage and no property,"[4] he was really a landowner of consequence in the region. After Colonel Ridgely died in 1791, the major quietly purchased his wife's birthplace along with thousands of additional acres when his father-in-law's estate was sold to discharge major debts.

Montpelier's relatively plain staircase, unostentatiously out of sight of the main entry, seems appropriate for the Quakers who built it. The Snowden family may have lined their austere hall with as many as forty-eight Windsor chairs.

The Snowdens raised five children at Montpelier, several of whom the informative nephew of George Washington described as "the handsomest children I ever beheld . . . [their talkativeness] seems to be hereditary as it has descended from the parents to the children—who are also as vociferous—and have as great volubility of tongue as par[r]ots."[5] Major Snowden's death in 1803 conveyed Montpelier to his wife; she lived there in the company of her son Nicholas and his family until her death in 1824.

Nicholas Snowden started the town of Laurel in 1811 with a gristmill and blacksmith's shop but, apparently at the behest of his mother, he moved his large family to Montpelier to live. It is the very thorough inventory made of Montpelier's contents at Nicholas Snowden's death in 1831 that provides the basis for furnishing five major rooms in the mansion's center block today: the dining room, parlor, hall, and two bedrooms. William Seale has stated in his "Montpelier, Project for the Interiors," prepared for the Maryland-National Capital Park and Planning Commission

A Brussels carpet, twelve hair bottom mahogany chairs, and one settee were part of the inventory of Montpelier's contents in the summer of 1831. Fashionable nineteenth-century decor would orchestrate a boldly printed wallpaper and white dimity fabric with such parlor furnishings.

Montpelier's restoration, begun in 1979, has been confined to the center block of the five-part Palladian structure. Additions and alterations in the early twentieth century have obliterated some traces of the original workmanship.

in February 1983, that ". . . the earliest full and useful document about the furnishings and use of Montpelier is the inventory of the son Nicholas in the summer of 1831, made nearly a century [*sic*] after Montpelier's construction."[6] Seale's plan furnishes the rooms with pieces comparable to those enumerated in the inventory and in keeping with the fashions of the times and the "plain" orientation of rural Quakers.

Montpelier was the home of the Snowdens and, by marriage, their Jenkins descendants until 1888. Between 1888 and its sale to the Maryland-National Capital Park and Planning Commission in 1961, the house changed hands seven times and lost, particularly in the wings, a good bit of its eighteenth-century configuration. Author William Pendleton and his wife owned the house from 1901 until 1912. Belgian Minister to the United States Emmanuel Havenith installed plumbing and built a kitchen in the service wing during his two-year residence beginning in 1916. Between 1928 and 1958, Assistant Secretary of State under Woodrow Wilson, Breckenridge Long, made Montpelier the cynosure of a handsome estate, noted for its thoroughbred horses, fine antiques, and warm hospitality. The King and Queen of the Belgians were his guests at Montpelier.

People of means owned Montpelier and protected its original features—moldings, mantels, paneling, and a large dining room cupboard with scalloped shelves. Using the zealous, new standards of early twentieth-century restoration, however, they also altered some of the interior architecture without leaving a trace of its original configuration. Rather than dismantle what was done, most notably after the house was renovated in 1918 by Eleanor Fitzgibbon of Pittsburgh, the Maryland-National Capital Park and Planning Commission has left the house undisturbed. Montpelier has served as a public facility for receptions since 1961. Placed on the National Register of Historic Places in 1970, five of its center block rooms are furnished to Nicholas Snowden's period of occupancy and function dually as museum and public reception rooms.

Hammond-Harwood House

Carved festoons of ribbons and roses adorn a doorway said to be the most beautifully conceived entrance on this side of the Atlantic. The five-part Palladian style house extends half the length of a city block and is considered one of the most perfect examples of Georgian architecture in America today.

In the more than two hundred years since its architect and its owner collaborated on the creation of the Hammond-Harwood House in Annapolis, paeans have celebrated its lovely design. Even in its own day, Mathias Hammond's town house was considered something of an architectural wonder. Both Thomas Jefferson and Charles Willson Peale made detailed sketches of it for their personal journals.

The Hammond-Harwood House was built between 1774 and 1775 by one of the finest architects of the period for an elegant, wealthy lawyer in Maryland's capital. Annapolis was then, as the Reverend Jonathan Boucher described, " . . . the genteelest town in North America and many of its inhabitants were highly respectable, as to station, fortune, and education."[1] Baron Ludwig Von Closen, aide-de-camp to the French General Rochambeau, found that "the wealthiest personages in the State have preferred to reside in Annapolis; hence the city contains a charming society and some very pretty women, very well bred, rather well dressed, and fond of entertainment."[2] Balls, concerts, and assemblies were de rigueur in the winter season for the city's elite, as was the ownership of a sumptuous residence.

One of the city's elite was Mathias Hammond, son and grandson of men who had served as President of His Lordship's Council. Only the wealthiest, most influential and established of landowners attained the prestigious office, and Mathias, elected to the Provincial Assembly for the first time in 1773 at the tender age of twenty-five, showed every indication of following in their footsteps.

Only months after his election, Hammond commissioned an architect to build a town house where he would reside while the Assembly was in session. There he planned to practice law, pursue his political career, and enjoy the endless rounds of social engagements Annapolis exacted from its leading citizens. He purchased two lots in the heart of fashionable Annapolis from his brother Denton and bargained with Edward Lloyd, who was building across the street, for two more. Construction at the northeast corner

The stately garden façade reiterates the prominent pediment of the front but introduces four great Doric pilasters of brick. This monumentality suggests a property of significant size and grandeur, like the Paca Gardens, at the rear.

of the large tract, subsequently known as Hammond's Square, commenced in the spring of 1774 with bricks made on one of the Hammond plantations.

The man Hammond chose to design and build his commodious residence was the bright new architect in town, the one who did the splashy interior for Edward Lloyd's house and the one whose familiarity with the latest London design trends had secured him the patronage of Maryland's and Virginia's premier families. William Buckland was a master builder; he was also a man of genius whose natural talent outstripped his early training in London as an apprentice to the Worshipful Company of Joiners.

Having immigrated to Virginia in 1755 at the age of twenty-one, Buckland worked as an indentured servant directing all the carpentry and joinery for the construction of George Mason's house, Gunston Hall. Then, lured to Annapolis in 1771, he established his reputation as a gentleman architect with a host of important commissions from leading Annapolitans. Although Gunston Hall exhibits a sublime grasp for one so young of the latest Georgian style in the Palladian manner, Buckland's Annapolis work had that ineffable extra: an originality evolved from his thorough understanding of the architectural pattern books of the day. The Hammond-Harwood House represents the culmination of Buckland's style. It was the most completely realized project of his life and marked him as "the finest architectural intelligence of the colonial years."[3]

The five-part design for Hammond's brick house was based on theories published by the sixteenth-century Italian architect Andrea Palladio and is successful because Buckland imbued the austere plan with refined proportions and magnificent details. Its perfection was not lost on Thomas Jefferson whose drawing of the five-part façade on Maryland Avenue was done to scale. Twentieth-century observers might miss the architectural subtleties for more obvious attractions. Ornamental details like the carved cartouche of the bull's-eye window in the pediment and the elaborately carved front entrance stand out against the plain surfaces and simple lines of English Palladianism. Seen in the full light of late afternoon, the entrance with its Ionic portico, garlanded spandrels, delicate fanlight, and archway defined by an egg and dart molding is at once an invitation to enter and a promise of inestimable beauty within.

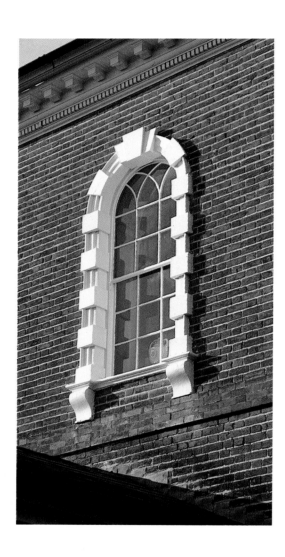

The rusticated window lighting the house's interior staircase was adapted by Buckland from James Gibbs's 1728 Book of Architecture.

The perfection of architect William Buckland's
1774 design for Mathias Hammond's town
house in Annapolis captivated the foremost
amateur architect of the day, Thomas Jefferson.
He made a scale drawing of the building's
refined proportions and magnificent details for
his personal journal as he stood across the street
from it.

Worthy of homage is the exquisitely conceived and carved front entrance. Architectural historians have described it as without equal in America. The floral swag in the spandrels over the fanlight is at once a lovely invitation to enter and a promise of beauty within.

What Buckland wrought inside Mr. Hammond's town house is at least as surprising as it is lovely. Instead of a reception hall and staircase in the full-blown formality of the Palladian style, the front door opens to a modest hall with a simple, elegant stair to one side. From the small hallway, a delightfully asymmetrical arrangement of rooms unfolds that is more typical of the neoclassical tenets of Robert Adam (all the rage in London at the time) than the theories of Palladio. The unorthodox layout allowed Buckland to place the most formal rooms, the drawing room and the dining room, at the rear of the house and one over top of the other presumably to give Hammond's guests the benefit of his spectacular view. In 1774, Hammond may have had as many as four garden terraces sloping away from the back of his house. Beyond them were Mr. Paca's wilderness garden, Mr. Brice's side garden, and farther off, like a cerulean backdrop to the parklike landscape, the Severn River and broad Chesapeake Bay.

As precocious as the layout of the house was for its time (the Adam influence would not flower in America until after the Revolution), the individual rooms fulfill every expectation for the highly formal, supremely balanced Georgian style popular in the colonies circa 1775. Rich ornamental plaster- and woodwork adorn the large rooms intended for the reception of Hammond's guests. Patterns of Baroque style arabesques decorate friezes over the doors, windows, and fireplace of the large dining room on the first floor. The two lovely dining room doors on either side of the fireplace are identical except that one of them opens onto a brick wall and was never intended for use. Buckland designed a door there merely to balance the room and complete its perfect Palladian symmetry!

He also disguised a door in one of the three dining room windows, and it is undetectable but for its bolt closure. The "jib door" provides a graceful, whimsical access to the garden when the wainscot below the window opens out like double doors, and the lower sash is simultaneously raised. Jib doors were not uncommon in eighteenth-century Annapolis. Buckland just put the device to uncommonly practical and aesthetic use. He needed a functioning door on the exterior garden façade, and he needed a window for the interior dining room design scheme. Ingeniously, he got both.

Adjoining the large drawing room that accommodated dancing and musicales is a small room for entertaining called the game room. Loo and whist were played at the circa 1750 English table installed in the room.

Hammond almost certainly entrusted Buckland with the entire design and execution of his house. Possibly, he extended his gifted architect carte blanche as well. Whatever their business relationship, in less than two years, it produced one of the most significant landmarks of the late colonial period in America. Tragically, however, the two men never derived the full measure of joy from their work. William Buckland died in November 1774 of unknown causes at the age of forty. He never saw the completion of his finest work. Mathias Hammond lost his 1776 bid for reelection to the Maryland General Assembly and retired abruptly to one of his country properties the year after the

The largest and finest room in the house is the
dining room with its rich carving and plasterwork of arabesques and modillions. The Maryland Federal dining table and six chairs and
portraits by Charles Willson Peale belonged to
the house's last owners, the Harwoods. William
Harwood's great-grandfather, whose portrait
appropriately hangs in the dining room, was
architect Buckland.

house was finished. He may have been bitterly disappointed with political life after his peers in Assembly ousted him for wanting to extend the vote to all men bearing arms for their country regardless of wealth and landholdings. Too, he may have found his luxurious new house superfluous during Revolutionary War time and obsolete afterwards when Annapolis went into a decline. Whatever the reason for his abrupt departure from Annapolis, no papers or contemporary references indicate he ever lived in his new house. In 1786, ten years after retiring from a public life which included membership on Maryland's Committees of Safety and Correspondence, the rank of quartermaster in the Severn Battalion of the county militia, exhibition of patriotic zeal in the Peggy Stewart Affair, and participation as vestryman in St. Anne's Church, Mathias Hammond died on his plantation, Howard's Adventure, in Gambrills. He was thirty-eight years old.

After changing hands four times in twenty-five years, Buckland's masterwork devolved on a family which not only kept it for more than a century but also descended directly from Buckland. William Harwood, Buckland's great-grandson, maintained the house in pristine condition despite the Civil War and reduced circumstances. Although he and his daughters after him had to sell off most of the property surrounding the house and rent out rooms inside, they managed to keep intact the magnificent interiors and an awesome assemblage of Harwood family heirlooms. No less than four Charles Willson Peale portraits of family ancestors graced their hallowed halls, including a handsome likeness of hazel-eyed William Buckland commissioned by the architect just before he died, then finished thirteen years later at the request of Buckland's daughter. It is an invaluable document, for beneath the architect's elbow Peale painted a plan and elevation of the Hammond-Harwood House, establishing for all time Buckland's part in the creation of the great house.

The only tinkering the Harwoods ever did to their beloved abode was to remove an elaborate mantel from the fireplace of the withdrawing room for the room's conversion to a kitchen in the 1880s. Sixty years later, the mantel was found where they had stored it, in the attic. So great was the Harwoods' pride in their house that "improvements" were never made. Consequently, restoration of the

ABOVE: *The ingenious jib door was disguised as a window, undetectable but for its bolt closure, in the formal first-floor dining room. Buckland designed the wainscoting to open outward and the window's lower sash to retract into a slot above.*

BELOW: *The jib door at the very center of the back of the house provided access to Mathias Hammond's terraced gardens and an overlook of Annapolis harbor.*

The parlor chamber or master bedroom displays a Baltimore Federal four poster bed with a tobacco and bellflower motif on the reeded posts. The doll featured in the Charles Willson Peale portrait of little Ann Proctor of Baltimore in 1789 is seated in the high chair beneath it.

structure, which retained nearly all its original window-panes, floors, and brass hardware, was never necessary.

When the last family member, Hester Ann Harwood, died in 1924 without a will, the contents of the house, appallingly, were sold at auction. Public concern, however, over the disposition of the house not only saved it from a dubious fate but also ignited a preservationist fervor in Annapolis that is unabated more than half a century later. Since 1926, the landmark has been a museum of the decorative arts furnished to reflect how a man of Hammond's stature would have lived in the eighteenth century. The Hammond-Harwood House Association, which purchased the house in 1940 from St. John's College, administers to the building and a collection of eighteenth-century furnishings (many of which belonged to the house prior to the 1924 auction) featuring the exceptional work produced in Maryland between 1760 and 1800. Under the association's able tutelage, the house is now designated a Historic Landmark on the National Register of Historic Places and a cynosure of Annapolis' National Historic Landmark District.

Breaking with Georgian tradition in the colonies, Buckland placed the important formal drawing room on the second floor, in part, perhaps, to give Hammond's guests the benefit of the lovely window views to the harbor. The English Chippendale brocade sofa is reputed to have been used by Washington at Valley Forge.

Hampton Mansion

When Rebecca Dorsey Ridgely arrived at the "Large, New Building" which was to be her home, she was overcome by "a desire to be more Devoted to the Lord . . ." and promptly went to prayers.[1]

Subsequent manor mistresses proved no less taken with their colossal abode. Eliza Ridgely combed the world's marketplaces for furnishings commensurate with the grandeur of her residence: English chandeliers, French candelabra, Italian paintings, and room-size "Turkey" carpets. Margaretta Ridgely entertained 1,500 for tea. Helen Ridgely, who likened the mansion to "the castle of some feudal lord," organized the Maryland Hunt Cup across the fields of the estate.

Since 1790, Hampton Mansion has set a standard for magnificence in American manorial living. Not even the twentieth-century passing of the princely Ridgelys from Hampton's halls has diminished its reputation. Superlatives still apply.

The National Park Service, which manages Hampton National Historic Site, states in its Historic Structure Report of 1980 that Hampton Mansion "is one of seventy-one outstanding examples of Georgian architecture still in existence in the United States. Its opulence has survived to the present, virtually intact . . ."[2] Not to be underestimated is the site's importance as an agricultural and industrial empire which remained in the control of one family for more than two hundred years. Today, twenty-three of the site's more than thirty-five original dependencies survive, offering a glimpse of life on a great working plantation before its decline in the late nineteenth century.

The sight of Hampton on its Baltimore County hilltop, surrounded by sixty acres of garden and greensward, is a shock for the unsuspecting motorist meandering along the suburban lanes north of Towson. If the grounds appear prodigious today, however, the onlooker might try imagining the estate with its original perimeters. It is said that Captain Charles Ridgely could ride twenty-seven miles across his property. At the time of his death, he had amassed 24,000 acres. A century later, descendants were still inheriting his land in Baltimore and Harford counties.

Captain Ridgely was fourth in a line of enterprising New World Ridgelys. Beginning with English emigré and barrister Robert who became Deputy of the Province and acting Attorney General circa 1670, the Ridgelys managed

Splendid Hampton Mansion ten miles north of Baltimore was begun in 1783 when wolves roamed the countryside. Its stuccoed and rusticated exterior simulated the building materials of a European country house. Nine period rooms currently on exhibit relate nearly two centuries of the social and aesthetic history of the prominent Ridgely family.

Several of Eliza Ridgely's marble urns purchased for Hampton in Europe in the mid-nineteenth century adorn the north porch.

A journal kept by Eliza Ridgely's daughter in 1841 and 1842 is preserved on the bookshelf of an English secretary in the master bedchamber. "I had six fights or wrestlings. Three with Isabel and three with Lizzy in all of which I laid them flat." Eliza, Jr.'s, boisterous girlhood at Hampton included snowball fights in the great hall.

to be in the right places at the right times throughout Maryland history. Charles the Planter was ensconced in Anne Arundel County when that county was the richest in the province. Charles the Merchant bought into Baltimore County when it was frontier and established the Northampton Furnace and Forges in partnership with his two sons. Younger son Captain Charles the Builder assumed control over the productive ironworks at the death of his brother, maintaining as well lucrative interests in his own mills, quarries, plantations, and a general merchandising business in Baltimore.

For sixty years, iron ore was a chief source of Ridgely wealth. Ridgely-owned furnaces supplied the Continental Army with armaments, and contributed to the growth of the family's successful mercantile business. Enormous profits, parlayed into fledgling enterprises such as horse racing and breeding, built one of America's earliest and most long-lived agricultural-industrial-commercial conglomerates. Appropriately, Captain Charles's iron ore profits also built the fabulous Hampton, and when the iron ore ran out, Northampton Furnace, now covered by the waters of Lock Raven Reservoir, provided a spectacular sight from the mansion's lofty cupola.

At the time of its construction, 1783–1790, Hampton Mansion was called Ridgely's Folly. Wolves roamed the wilderness. The nearest neighbors were cabin dwellers who could ill afford the price of a warming stove. A paucity of local gentry discouraged the influx of fashion. Yet Captain Ridgely was a tycoon, a representative for nearly seventeen straight years in the Maryland House of Delegates, and the acknowledged political boss of Baltimore County. His burgeoning wealth could easily underwrite the building of a palace in the boondocks.

Until recently, the majestic cupola atop Hampton Mansion was thought to be a replica of the octagonal dome on Castle Howard in England. Charles Ridgely, so the legend goes, displayed his kinship with the English Howards by copying their cupola. More probably, the idea originated with Ridgely's carpenter-architect, Jehu Howell. On a flyleaf of a 1787 account book, Ridgely wrote a note: "When I gave Mr. Howell leave to put on the Dome of my house, the expense to me was not to exceed £180 . . ."3 Charles Ridgely indulged in luxuries, but flamboyance had a limit.

Jehu Howell *may* have been the architect of Hampton.

The music room is furnished to represent the Ridgely occupancy during the latter half of the nineteenth and early twentieth centuries. The harp belonged to Eliza Ridgely between 1803 and 1867 and was reputedly played for Lafayette. It was ordered by Eliza's father from London for $600.

Charles Carnan Ridgely once hosted a ball for 300 guests in Hampton Mansion's great hall. Among them were Baltimore ladies destined to become sisters-in-law of Europe's formidable Napoleon Bonaparte and the Duke of Wellington. A rare, complete set of Baltimore painted furniture, circa 1815, owned by John Eager Howard, lines the room. A copy of Thomas Sully's Lady with a Harp *pays homage to Hampton's celebrated chatelaine, Eliza Ridgely. At fifteen years old, she was an accomplished harpist whose portrait with the harp was reproduced on playing cards of the day.*

Captain Ridgely, himself, *could* have been the architect as was the custom of those gentlemen of the period who had architectural books in their libraries. Since original plans for the building have never been found, the identity of the architect is a mystery. Whoever he was, he designed one of the largest eighteenth-century houses in Maryland, a record which stood until the midnineteenth century.

The design of Hampton conforms to the Georgian formula for a five-part classically inspired Palladian great house. The plan, which included a large central hall in the main block flanked by extended wings, was popular circa 1750 in England and the American colonies, specifically among the upper classes for their estates, where "show" was considered indispensable. Captain Ridgely utilized this older style when he built his country house after the Revolutionary War; in coming into his vast new fortune, he may have been anxious to establish himself with an earlier, well-respected architectural aesthetic. Too, his predilection for an older style may have been one of taste. His travels as a mariner on his father's ships to England, and to Annapolis and Philadelphia as a Maryland delegate, would have introduced him to the finest Georgian architecture.

Although the use of stucco, "rusticated" to look like cut stone, was a sophisticated technique more common to Europe than Maryland, Hampton's two-story wings, promi-

The dining room has been carefully researched to the 1815–1829 period of Charles Carnan Ridgely's residence at Hampton. The ornate window treatments were deduced from patterns of the time and Ridgely's inventory for three pairs of blue silk curtains with yellow and blue silk draperies. The portrait of the first Mrs. Ridgely of Hampton by Hesselius is hung high on the wall in the style of the time.

nent porticos, and less-than-pristine Palladian proportions are not the mark of a formally trained architect. Whatever his breach of Georgian architectural etiquette, the unidentified architect of Hampton built a house that would accommodate the Ridgelys for six generations.

The new house was not yet painted inside when the captain died. He was fifty-seven years old and childless. His heir apparent was his nephew, brother-in-law, and business associate, Charles Carnan. Thirty-year-old Carnan had only to satisfy one condition in his uncle's will to inherit a fortune: change his name. With alacrity he obliged. By act of the Maryland Legislature of 1790, Charles Ridgely Carnan became Charles Carnan Ridgely. Rebecca, the captain's widow, inherited Hampton, but, in an agreement of January 1791, she decided to exchange the house and all interests therein for Auburn, a dwelling which originally stood on the grounds of the present campus of Towson State University.

Charles Ridgely and his wife Priscilla (younger sister by twenty-three years of Rebecca Ridgely) celebrated their acquisition of Hampton with no let-up in the hard work instigated by the captain. The large, elegant rooms in the main block, so obviously intended for lavish entertaining, were no enticement to fritter away the captain's fortune. Instead, Charles Ridgely undertook in April 1791 extensive interior painting with colors such as "Prussian Bleu, Verdigrease Green, Patent Yellow, and Litherage of Gold."[4] He ordered furnishings that included quantities of oilcloth floor coverings, presumably to protect the captain's exquisitely made pine floors, and had "landskips" painted in one or more of the decorative overmantels in the four principal parlors. He hired gardeners to landscape Hampton's stark hilltop: On three terraces at the south façade constructed earlier by the captain (in what has been described as the largest earth-moving project for any early American garden), Charles Ridgely designated six formal parterres, then between 1798 and 1801 had an irrigation system of wooden pipes installed to convey water to the house and to a magnificent "falling" garden. The result of his horticultural efforts, embellished by later generations, inspired one visitor to write: "It has been truly said of Hampton that it expresses more grandeur than any other place in America."[5]

As if the installations of the mammoth new abode and operation of the plantation and Ridgely business interests were not enough for the new master, Charles Carnan Ridgely was also a brigadier general in the state militia by 1796, a director of two Baltimore banks, a member of the board of the Baltimore College of Medicine, a catalyst in establishing the B&O Railroad, a member of the Maryland Legislature (1790–1795) and the state Senate (1796–1800), and Governor of Maryland (1815–1818). His wife Priscilla pursued somewhat more specialized avenues of interest. She converted to Methodism and raised eleven of their more than thirteen children beyond infancy.

The vigorous Ridgely family thrived at Hampton under Charles "The General" Ridgely's capable direction. He was a renowned host, including Charles Carroll of Carrollton

Grained mahogany doors and closely matched pine floorboards are indicative of the great care and expense that went into the building of Hampton.

in one guest list of 300, impressing an English author with his keeping "the best table in America," and utilizing, in the best British tradition, the great hall for banquets and balls. His stables housed the fastest thoroughbreds of the time. His fields were models of cultivation. Upon his death in 1828, his 312 slaves were either freed or "provided for comfortably during their old age at the general charge of my Estate, to be borne in equal contribution by all my children and grandchildren."[6]

The general made Hampton every bit the cynosure his uncle had planned for. In keeping with the intention of the National Park Service to return Hampton's exhibit rooms to different periods in the Ridgely family history, the dining room on the southeast corner of the main block has been restored to the circa 1810–1829 period of the general's occupancy. The master bedchamber is furnished to the earliest period of occupancy, from 1790 to 1814, while the drawing room, always considered the finest room in the

The Ridgely coat of arms was installed in stained glass in the fanlights over the doors at either end of the great hall.

Carpenter Jehu Howell's bills for building Hampton totaled more than £3,482 before his death in 1787. The cost of the great octagonal cupola atop the house was not, by order of owner Charles Ridgely, supposed to exceed £180.

house by generations of Ridgelys, reflects today the domain of the general's son John and his illustrious wife Eliza from the period of their occupancy, 1829–1867. The "modern" taste of this third generation at Hampton is reflected in the exquisite furnishings gathered internationally to complement the furniture and silver produced by Baltimore's world-class craftsmen.

Family legend recounts that Eliza played the harp in the music room for Lafayette in 1824 and so entranced the French gentleman that he initiated a correspondence with her that lasted the rest of his life. Before she married John Ridgely, as a fifteen-year-old boarding school student in Philadelphia in 1818, she had her full-length portrait with her harp painted by Thomas Sully. The likeness, exhibited at the Pennsylvania Academy of Fine Arts when it was finished, cost $500 and later became a popular motif for calendars and playing cards of the day. *Lady with a Harp* went to the National Gallery of Art in 1945, but a fine copy is now displayed in the great hall where the original hung for one hundred years.

Eliza's legacy to Hampton was her great style and the fortune her merchant father lavished on his only child. Her forty marble vases, purchased in Europe, still punctuate the garden walkways, and a cedar of Lebanon seedling she purportedly carried out of the Middle East in a shoe box and planted on the south lawn is now a giant of national standing. Although Hampton's assets flourished through Eliza's tenure as mistress, in spite of the Civil War and the necessity to replace slaves with servants, the estate was reduced progressively by division among the heirs. By 1872, Hampton Mansion and its grounds comprised approximately 1,000 acres. In 1929, Hampton's fifth master sold the mansion's wine cellar to J. P. Morgan and used the profits to install electricity. Finally, in 1945, the upkeep of the mansion, grounds, farm, and outbuildings became untenable, and in 1948 Hampton Mansion, 43.29 acres, and a portion of its magnificent furnishings were acquired by the National Park Service.

Far from being a tragic dénouement to Hampton's long and fruitful history, the sale of the estate at well below fair market value to the Avalon Foundation, which presented it to the National Park Service, insured its preservation. What's more, the designation of Hampton as a National Historic Site on June 22, 1948, marked the first time the National Park Service had acquired a historic property for its architectural value. This milestone in cooperative efforts between government and the private sector inspired the small group of people who worked to save Hampton to go on and form the National Trust for Historic Preservation. According to one key member of the fledgling trust, the success and all ramifications of Hampton's purchase can be laid at the feet of *Lady with a Harp*. Eliza Ridgely's portrait, hanging in Hampton's great hall, had not only impressed philanthropists as an example of the work of Thomas Sully worthy of purchase for the National Gallery; it had also led to discussions with John Ridgely, Jr., that would forever preserve one of America's premier residences.

Union Mills Homestead

Organic continuity describes this house that grew from two joined log houses to a sprawling pastiche of almost two centuries of rural architecture, housing one vigorous family line. Walking past the white picket portals and across a brick courtyard, homey and dappled in the shade of mammoth trees, is like sleepwalking into someone else's dream.

Few houses have so documented, unbroken, and eventful a history as the Homestead at Union Mills, but then few families have had the vitality of the Shrivers. In their fourth generation of successful adaptation to the American frontier, they built a house that nurtured six more generations.

Andrew, born Schreiber in 1673, in the German Palatinate village of Alsenborn, emigrated to America. He settled beside the Schuylkill River in Pennsylvania in 1721 at the age of forty-eight with his German wife, their children, and her children from a first marriage.

The second Andrew Schreiber was his parents' firstborn, and he evinced traits that established a familial pattern for success. As soon as he was twenty-one, he obtained his freedom from indenture and left his father's home. He paid for his first piece of property with shoes: for each pair of "negro shoes" he made Mr. John Digges, he received an acre of "Digges' Choice" bottomland beside Conewago Creek on the Maryland-Pennsylvania border.[1] He made one hundred pairs of shoes.

To clear the land and plant corn, he enlisted the aid of his half-brother David and uncannily set in motion a habit of fraternal cooperation that reverberated through several ensuing generations. Only when the Civil War turned brother against brother was the extraordinary pattern of David and Andrew altered in the Shriver family.

Interesting to note is Andrew's penchant for observation revealed in the family genealogy book of 1888. He notes his drive was through "grass as high as the wagon to get to the new place" and documents that "the marks of passage were visible there for several years."[2] *Schreiber* in German signifies a writer; subsequent Schreibers would produce a record of observations second in volume only to the Adams family of Boston.

David, Andrew's son, dressed in deerskins until he was fifteen and watched Delaware and Catawba Indians refresh themselves at the farm's limestone well after their raiding

forays against neighboring tribes every spring. He educated his children in English, was elected to the Maryland
Legislature, serving there for thirty years, and helped
frame the U.S. Constitution in 1776. David Shriver was the
family patriarch on Little Pipe Creek in Maryland responsible for anglicizing the Schreiber name.

Great gains in each generation culminated in the fourth
with the construction in 1797 of the house and mill complex that came to be the Union Mills Homestead. Appropriately, of David's eight children, Andrew (born 1762) and
David (born 1769) were the instigators. They ambitiously
bought land from an estate for which their father was executor on Big Pipe Creek in what was then Frederick
County. The Land Act of 1796 had apparently suggested

*The house was remodeled as the little town of
Union Mills grew prosperous. When the
Shrivers purchased a franchise for the Bal-
timore-Pittsburgh stagecoach to stop, they made
a public dining room of one side of joined log
houses the brothers had built in 1797. The
massive one-piece poplar corner cupboard was
probably made for the room. One of the Homestead's last owners installed the leaded glass bay
window.*

Andrew Shriver's help in electing Thomas Jefferson to the presidency is supposed to have garnered his postmastership of the locality. He worked from the little desk.

Paneled shutters frame a window in the oldest section of the house. The evolution of the Homestead can be traced through architectural elements corresponding to different periods of construction.

opportunity to them along the road joining Baltimore to Pennsylvania and points west. "Purchase a few hundred acres of land [on the Monocacy River], lay off a town and commence trade there,"[3] urged a prescient friend from Georgetown in 1793.

Andrew gave up his store and tannery in Littlestown, Pennsylvania, and David sold his Westminster mill, to meet, as the story goes, and pool their interests at this halfway point. They built two mills: a gristmill for the grain they would grow, and a sawmill to process the timber and oak bark necessary for tanning leather. Work from the two mills eventually generated a host of enterprises including a farm, tannery, granary, cooperage, blacksmithy, cannery, store, post office, inn, tavern, stagecoach stop, and school. The thriving settlement that sprang from the union of two mills and two brothers was a prototype for the American industrial park.

Within twenty-four hours of contracting for the mills to be built, Andrew and David drew up the January 26, 1797, contract: ". . . in consideration of One Hundred pounds . . . to . . . Henry Kohlstock . . . to finish two small houses fourteen by seventeen feet each to be connected by a porch & passage about 10 feet wide . . ."[4] The small double house was, essentially, two log cabins sheathed in clapboard and

In their fourth generation of successful adaptation to America, the Shriver family built a homestead that nurtured six more generations. It grew from two rooms in 1797 to more than twenty-three in the nineteenth century.

In June 1863 before the Battle of Gettysburg, the Union Army came down the pike and swarmed through the orchard and across the backyard to the Homestead where they received a warm welcome from Union sympathizer Andrew Shriver.

connected by a dogtrot, or passage, with a communal staircase between. The passage may have been open on both ends, but it was roofed and spanned at the front façade by a two-story porch.

Why did the brothers agree to share the staircase and porch in a house with identically small rooms on upper and lower floors? Finances may have dictated that the dwelling be small when the gristmill was so much larger and more substantially built. Practicality certainly guided the brothers' less-than-picturesque siting of the house only sev-

The proximity of the milling workplace to the Homestead encouraged the Shrivers' strong work ethic and the growth of an industrial complex in the yard. The brothers' milling enterprise is credited as the forerunner of the modern American industrial park.

eral hundred yards from the mill: They didn't waste land they could farm by building on it. Too, sharing was less a burden to these enterprising siblings than a means to more successful ends.

The modest four-room house stood autonomous for about two decades with merely a kitchen outbuilding to answer the needs of at least one growing Shriver household. David was a twenty-eight-year-old bachelor when he moved in. Thirty-five-year-old Andrew, however, brought a wife and six children and accrued five more offspring in time.

By 1803, David had left his portion of the dwelling to engineer the construction of the Reisterstown Pike. His departure ironically led to the house becoming more crowded. The road he built brought travelers to the inn Andrew opened in the vacated rooms and farmers to the mills. Political influence came with growth, and Andrew was appointed postmaster for the burgeoning hamlet by President Jefferson.

At about this time, the open-air passage between the log houses may have been enclosed and a new staircase and stair hall installed to make a formal entrance for the house. Legend has it the Chinese Chippendale balustrade embellishing both the interior staircase and the balcony on the porch outside copied the porch and roof railings at Monticello. Political stumping for the German vote was heavy at the Shriver house in election years, and Andrew Shriver asserted his zealous allegiance to Thomas Jefferson in the distinctive platform he erected on the house for speechifying.

David relinquished his business interests in the mills following a prestigious appointment in 1811 secured for him by Andrew in Washington as superintendent of the National Road west of Cumberland. Presumedly, Andrew was free to remodel after 1811. He was nearing fifty years old and most of his eleven children still lived cheek-by-jowl in the house that harbored an inn, tavern, school, store, magistrate's office, and post office. Probably by 1820 he enlarged the rooms of the log house on the west, then attached a substantial addition connecting the house to the primitive kitchen building out back.

The Shrivers still refer to the enlarged west room of the original log structure as the "dancing room" and the ground-floor room of the circa 1820 addition as the "dining room." When, in the 1830s, Andrew purchased a franchise

The gristmill that the Shriver brothers built in 1797 stimulated the growth of their town, Union Mills. They built the grist- and sawmills first, then contracted for the double log houses that became Union Mills Homestead.

A great-great-grandson of Andrew Shriver opened the Homestead and its priceless collections of family memorabilia to visitors in 1967. RIGHT: *The small Homestead kitchen was a Confederate mob scene in the early hours of June 30, 1863, as the Shrivers' cook fed hundreds of Jeb Stuart's cavalrymen en route to Gettysburg.*

for the stagecoach to stop enroute to Pittsburgh, the dancing room was a public room for travelers. One notable wayfarer, Washington Irving, took his ease by a stove on a cold Saturday night and talked to old Andrew until midnight. John James Audubon paused at "The Mills" on his travels across the country enlisting charter subscribers to *The Birds of America.* He made a note of the romantic old place and the Baltimore orioles nesting in the great trees around the old building by the creek.

Additions to the east façade were not undertaken until after Andrew's death in 1847. Four sons moved away and brought the family distinction by developing Maryland's highways, waterways, and railroads west. Two sons stayed home and inherited a partnership in the mills and farm. Andrew Keiser Shriver assumed management of the tannery and lived, as he always had, in his father's house while William operated the gristmill from a house he built across the road in 1826. At this time, the name of the Shrivers' home place changed. Known as the Mills until old Andrew died, the house became the Homestead between 1847 and 1850.

The 1860s might be considered the most representative and exciting period in the Homestead's long history. With twenty-three rooms, six fireplaces, and a new wing appended to the northeast for extended family use, the dwelling had reached its final sprawling dimensions. A rift in family philosophy, caused by William's marriage to a Catholic girl and subsequent affiliation with local Democrats, elicited rancorous mutterings from Andrew at the Homestead. At the birth of William's thirteenth child, Andrew announced, "He should have named the last one 'Enough'!"[5] The stage was set for trouble on the eve of the Civil War.

"I am a Union Man,"[6] wrote Andrew K. Shriver as he sent two sons to war and eleven slaves to freedom following the Emancipation Proclamation. William, who never owned slaves, sent four sons to fight for the Confederacy. Unlike most families divided by the Civil War, the Shrivers endured a galling test of their loyalties: They were visited in rapid succession by the Union and Confederate armies, friend to one brother and foe to the other.

With aplomb, Andrew K.'s household endured the depredations of hundreds of scavenging Confederate cavalrymen on June 30, 1863, while their general, Jeb Stuart, took a leisurely breakfast across the road in brother William's house. As fast as "old black" Ruth Dohr could pour flapjacks onto the griddle in the old fireplace, the soldiers snatched them up to eat half-cooked. Horses were taken and leather stolen from the tannery; General Stuart reimbursed Andrew K. with one dollar Confederate tender.

Within hours of Stuart's departure, the Federal troops of Sykes's Fifth Corps came marching down the hill to the Homestead. General Barnes was promptly offered the finest guest room and his officers sleeping space on the porches as they made the Homestead their temporary headquarters. The three young Shriver ladies entertained the officers with music on the Steinway piano in the dancing room and left their impression of the evening written on the back of an envelope with the names of the seven officers. Meanwhile, William's sixteen-year-old son Herbert was guiding the Confederate cavalry north into Pennsylvania where they would eventually meet the Union army at the battle of Gettysburg.

Divided loyalties came to a frosty dénouement in the next generation as Shriver cousins gradually overcame their antagonisms. Andrew's son and William's daughter, occupying their fathers' houses across the road from each other, finally spoke to one another nearly a half-century after the Civil War!

With the Civil War the pattern broke: The Homestead was owned by three brothers instead of two. Andrew K. Shriver's three sons continued to produce fine leather while

Porch space was commodious on the rear façade and quite common on nineteenth-century houses of the area. In summertime, sleeping was comfortable on the elevated, open breezeways.

The Chinese Chippendale railing on one second-story porch is said to indicate Andrew Shriver's political ties to Thomas Jefferson, who used the motif at Monticello.

William Shriver's sons moved their cannery to Westminster. With the slow attrition of family members and few children coming up in the ranks, the roomy old Homestead became something of a white elephant at the beginning of the twentieth century. Older portions of the house gathered occasional guests, servants, and volumes of memorabilia. The 1860s addition with its fine Victorian parlor and breakfast room was the last and somewhat abated hub of the famous Shriver family activity. By 1940, only one nonagenarian son of Andrew K. and a seventy-year-old niece remained in the house. In 1942, the old gristmill ceased operation. The Union Mills Homestead Foundation was established in 1964 to preserve and maintain the site.

In 1970 the house was placed on the National Register of Historic Places. The finest award for its longevity, however, must be the poem by Samuel Shriver entitled "The Homestead," a portion of which reads:

> . . . that stately old mansion,
> Of which we make boast as this home,
> With its staunch o'ershadowing trees,
> Arching the lawn like a dome.
>
> It was built by and sheltered our sires,
> The children and grandchildren too,
> Who ever found heartiest welcome,
> Returning their love to renew.[7]

I have been all through Lord Littleton's Palace even to the kitchen and it is more like the old castles we read of in novels than anything else—vaulted passages, arched doorways and private staircases . . . It is really a curiosity.

Teackle Mansion

So wrote young Elizabeth Waters of her visit to Littleton Dennis Teackle's mansion in Princess Anne on July 31, 1811.[1] Her words were no exaggeration or figment of a girl's imagination. They identify an air of mystery and romance that pervades the abode Mr. Teackle modeled after a Scottish manor house in 1801. Decades later, Teackle Mansion actually became the setting for a novel: George Alfred Townsend based his best-selling novel *The Entailed Hat* on the financial ruin of Mr. Teackle and the subsequent entailment of his fabulous residence.

Few houses capture the public's fancy and achieve immortality in fiction. In the grand tradition of *The House of Seven Gables,* the house at the end of Prince William Street inspired a story as astonishing as what actually happened behind its doors in the first half of the nineteenth century. Attribute the novel's achievement, in part, to Teackle Mansion's beauty.

The five-part, salmon-colored brick "pile" with pale wood trim was regal in its day behind a high iron fence. Novelist Townsend would have stood outside its fancy grille gate looking across lawns dotted with "forest trees . . . a great willow, and some tawny cedars, and bushes of rose and lilac"[2] to record for his book and for posterity the appearance of Teackle Mansion:

It was nearly two hundred feet in length, and would have made three respectable churches, standing in line, with their sharp gables to the front . . .

Its central gable had deep carved eaves . . . The two mighty chimneys of that centre were parallel with the ridge of the roof . . . bespeaking four great fireplaces below . . .

. . . A doorway, opening on a low, open portico platform with steps, seemed to say to visitors: "Men of port and consideration come in this way, but inferiors enter by some of the smaller doors!"[3]

The house was started circa 1801 but was not even completed eight years later when a visitor to Teackle's mansion likened it to "the old castles we read of in novels . . ."

Interior windows with mirrored panes reflect light and garden views into the parlor. The mirror over the mantel came from Governor Ogle's house in Annapolis. Because of the way Littleton Teackle lost his mansion, very little remains that was original to his period of ownership.

Although much of the parklike setting and all the tall iron fencing was supplanted in the twentieth century by a street, the hauteur conveyed by the building's fine Federal lines is undiminished. Its large central block with a pedimented gable and bull's-eye window in the east façade is flanked symmetrically by long hyphens and two large two-story wings. A delicately molded pattern of urns and garlands is still elegant on three panels between the first and second stories of the central block.

It is a stately house, and since its reclamation in 1960 from apartments built around twenty-four original rooms and ten fireplaces, the myriad interconnecting passages, doorways, and staircases have again assumed the disorienting, mysterious ambience that so captivated the girl Elizabeth Waters. To walk Teackle's halls and see the drawing room's mirrored windows reflecting garden sunlight and the massive kitchen fireplace in the south wing deeply indented where slaves sharpened their cooking knives is to glimpse what was once the lifestyle nonpareil of an extraordinary gentleman.

Littleton Dennis Teackle made and lost at least one fortune in his lifetime. He came to Princess Anne from Ac-

Teackle Mansion was the setting for a best-selling nineteenth-century novel based loosely on the life of the man, Littleton Dennis Teackle, who built it. The rear façade overlooks gardens and a curve in the sleepy Manokin River.

comack County on Virginia's Eastern Shore with his wife, Elizabeth Upshur Teackle, between 1795 and 1800. He purchased eighteen acres of land known as Beckford Grant and started building his mansion in 1801. Legend has it he went abroad and brought back the plans of a ducal or baronial residence near Edinburgh, Scotland, for his Princess Anne residence. He appended the wings to the central block in 1803, and these, according to Elizabeth Waters's letter, "were not near completed" (probably on the inside) eight years later. A letter written by Teackle in 1806 to the London firm of Barclay and Salkeld discloses the ambition

Legend has it that Teackle, who made and lost at least one fortune in his lifetime, brought back the plans for his 1801 Eastern Shore mansion from Scotland.

and business acumen of this young man who started Teackle Mansion when he was only twenty-four years old.

> Having purchased their interests from my late Partners, and taken upon myself entirely the Business which formerly existed between my Father, my two Uncles (the Messrs Dennis's) and myself under the firm above mentioned . . . I have contemplated a Trade in Timber from this place to your town . . . My situation renders the discovery of a good market for Timber peculiarly interesting and important—Possessing Lands contiguous to navigation, I engaged with our government for the Supply of the Navy Department . . . you will perceive that advantages may be gained by shipments to Liverpool, predicated upon your quotations.[4]

Littleton Teackle's success with timber—supplying the American and British navies with ship spars, root knees, black walnut timber, "Navy Plank," and other naval materials—eventually grew to include his own mercantile fleet, a bank, and railroad interests. He was an entrepreneur extraordinaire who started life as the scion of a landowning family but whose ability to diversify catapulted him into the highest tier of society. He was the confidant of presidents and an innovator who brainstormed some of our country's most fundamental institutions. He is credited with starting the public school system during one of his stints in the Maryland Legislature. He opened the first commercial bank in Maryland (and perhaps in America), established Maryland's first commercial banking laws, and instigated the building of a railroad from Wilmington, Delaware, to the lower Eastern Shore of Maryland. At President Jefferson's suggestion, he is said to have supplied lumber for a fleet of "gunboats" to protect American harbors and mercantile interests during the War of 1812.

When part of his own fleet of mercantile ships was pillaged by Barbary pirates in the Mediterranean, Mr. Teackle's fortunes went into decline. His bank in Somerset County failed. He lost Teackle Mansion at least once, and only through the generosity of friends and family was he reinstated. He and his wife, however, resorted to raising vegetables to keep their family going, and when they finally lost Teackle Mansion for good, the U.S. Government auctioned it off to the highest bidder.

Elizabeth Upshur Teackle died in 1835 at the age of fifty-two. Her husband died in Baltimore in 1848, by all accounts, destitute. St. Andrew's Church in Princess Anne paid for the burial of his body, beside his wife's grave, in the small churchyard down the way from Teackle Mansion. Their monumental house changed hands several times between 1823, when the U.S. Circuit Court seized it, and 1851, when the property, including the house, was subdivided. In 1856, the Female Academy of Somerset County occupied the mansion's north end while Dr. John W. Dashiell and his wife lived in the central section and south wing. Eventually, Dr. Dashiell's spinster sisters acquired the north wing. In 1910, however, the two separate deeds to Teackle Mansion became three as the Dashiells entailed the house in three different bequests to three different family members. Dashiell descendants relinquished the central block

Double doors in the parlor lead to boxwood gardens and the river from which Teackle's fleet of mercantile ships sailed the world. When the fleet was pillaged by the Barbary pirates in the Mediterranean Sea, Teackle's fortunes declined. He was eventually forced to forfeit his home.

On the edge of the big kitchen fireplace are deep grooves where servants reputedly sharpened cooking knives.

and south wing in 1960 to Olde Princess Anne Days, a group dedicated to the restoration and preservation of Teackle Mansion. The north wing was sold to the Somerset County Historical Society which maintains its headquarters there.

Under the indefatigable ministrations of Maude Jeffries, Olde Princess Anne Days installed modern heating in Teackle Mansion, restored its intricate ceiling pargetting, acquired its National Register status, ushered in period furnishings, and galvanized the interest of state and local government, wealthy benefactors, and Teackle family descendants. In the twentieth century, serendipity has settled on Teackle Mansion. Littleton Dennis Teackle's great-grand-nephew came to Princess Anne several years ago on a lark to see the old place; his appearance coincided with a sudden, serious dearth of restoration funds. Overhearing the discussion about the matter taking place in the garden, the young man stepped forward. "I would be glad to help," he said and proffered a check for the needed amount. On another occasion, friends of the mansion lunching in New York City were overheard talking about the house by a woman sitting at the next table who was a Teackle descendant. She donated the family Bible to the mansion.

Today, the furnishings in the mansion do not duplicate "Lord Littleton's" milieu at the height of his success. For lack of inventories, no one knows how the Teackles furnished their rooms. Elizabeth Waters's letter, however, cites Mr. Teackle's stylish library and the housekeeper's apartments that were as large as a house of the period. The kitchen was outfitted with so many shelves, "it may be kept as neat as a drawing room." Its hearth and all around a newfangled "patent steam machine for cooking" were paved with marble. Some of the wonders Elizabeth observed are still extant in the mansion. In the north wing, adjoining what Miss Waters referred to as "Her Ladyship's lodging room," are Mr. and Mrs. Teackle's dressing closets, each with its own diminutive, cater-cornered fireplace. Between the two dressing closets is a room tiled with marble and inset with shelves. One heavy marble tile in the floor is removable and leads to a small underground cistern where bath water drained from the "very large marble bath" Elizabeth Waters observed there. At a time when bathing was done with difficulty from a portable tub, Mr. Teackle's ingenious bathing room was, like himself, ahead of its time.

Above Mr. and Mrs. Teackle's suite were the rooms of their only child, Elizabeth: a bedroom as large as their own with a spacious dressing closet and library adjoining it. Miss Waters must have looked with envy upon her contemporary, the daughter of wealthy parents, whose room was "to be papered with pink with the figure of Flora . . ." Years later when the Teackles were plagued by poverty, ignominious failure, and, perhaps, even undesired newspaper publicity, Elizabeth Teackle's life was not enviable. She owned Teackle Mansion for a period after the sale by the U.S. Government, but there are indications she sold off portions of her property to keep a roof over her parents' heads. Finally, in 1839, four years after her mother's death, Elizabeth Anne Upshur Teackle married at the age of thirty-eight. When the mirrored windows of the mansion's drawing room no longer reflected Teackle ships successfully plying the Manokin River from their overseas travels, she was not to mourn any more. She gave her father some of her Teackle property before she sold every bit of the rest of her interest in it. She married Aaron Quinby and removed to Accomack County, Virginia, where she is buried today on the fine estate of Warwick.

The story of Mr. Teackle and his fabulous residence is

A delicately molded pattern of urns and garlands is still elegant on a panel of the front façade.

laden with legend, shadows, half-truths, and hearsay. There are those who have heard tell Littleton Dennis Teackle trafficked in illegal slaves whom he smuggled into the mansion's basement via an underground tunnel from the river; that he bilked the government with the quality of timber he sold; that he had a reputation as a serious gambler. Whatever the truth, the sensational events of his life undoubtedly drew national attention and piqued the curiosity of novelist George Alfred Townsend.

Like Townsend, we might wish to color the shadowy lives of the Teackles with some happiness. We might wish to read fact into the fiction of *The Entailed Hat:* that the lovely only child of the master of "Teackle Hall" bears some resemblance to Littleton Dennis Teackle's daughter and that she tried to help her father regain his home. The fact is, however, Mr. Teackle experienced no happy ending to his story. We must be consoled that the restoration of the mansion represents the restoration of the spirit of the family who built it.

Teackle Mansion's central block and south wing are owned and maintained by Olde Princess Anne Days, an organization spearheaded by Maude Jeffries, whose portrait hangs in the south hall. The Somerset County Historical Society owns and maintains headquarters in the north wing.

My Dear Sir, I am induced by every motive of propriety, and by the respect which I owe to your feelings as a Father, to explain the real object of my frequent visits in your Family . . .

Homewood

Spirited words, written by Charles Carroll, Jr., in 1800 to Chief Justice Benjamin Chew of Pennsylvania, declare twenty-five-year-old Carroll's "unalterable affection" for the judge's daughter.[1]

Spirited, too, was the house he built following his marriage to Miss Harriet Chew with land and funds presented by his father, Charles Carroll of Carrollton. As tragic as Carroll's life turned in his later addiction to alcohol, the exuberance of youth found ultimate, enduring expression in the house he named Homewood.

It has been called sophisticated, refined, and elegant by architectural historians and is considered a diminutive version of the five-part Palladian plan for country house architecture that enthralled the British and American aristocracy before the Revolutionary War. Georgian-inspired but laden with rich, contemporaneous Adamesque details inside and out, Homewood was a synthesis at the time of its construction, 1801–1809, of the Georgian-Adamesque-Federal styles in Baltimore.

Like many country seats from Baltimore's prosperous Federal past, this two-room-deep, one-and-a-half-story central block with single-story wings and low connecting hyphens was built on a hill with a view toward Baltimore. Its tall, classically inspired portico was magnificent in the distance, ennobling a front (south) façade simply treated with long windows surmounted by inset sandstone panels.

Similarly beautiful Federal mansions, like Belvidere, were eliminated with the city's growth or adapted for reuse. Only Homewood survives intact and, since its restoration in 1987, reveals Baltimore's sumptuous Federal past and Charles Carroll, Jr.'s, personal vision for a genteel rural establishment.

Not everyone shared young Carroll's enthusiasm for his ambitious undertaking, and therein lies the most fascinating tale from Homewood's past. The person whose approbation was most expedient for Homewood's construction disapproved as the plans developed. Charles Carroll of Carrollton, indomitable patriarch and illustrious signer of

Country houses of the Federal period in Baltimore graced all the major hilltops affording prospects of the Patapsco River and distant Bay. Homewood's elongated, classical south portico emphasized its lofty status.

Homewood's restorers took their cue from the relatively simple carving on the fireplace that this room was intended less for entertaining than family use. The Sèvres tea service on the circa 1800 Maryland Pembroke table belonged to Betsy Patterson. The portrait of Daniel Carroll II of Upper Marlboro was painted circa 1760 by John Wollaston.

OPPOSITE: *Although no documentation has come to light designating specific uses for each room in Homewood, a bedroom such as this would have been reserved for Charles Carroll of Carrollton who liked to visit with his children's families for several weeks at a time. It is called the chintz chamber for the Portland chintz window and bed hangings documented at England's Victoria and Albert Museum to have been in use in 1790. The Federal carved mahogany high post bed with bed steps is believed to have belonged to Charles Carroll.*

the Declaration of Independence, whom John Adams once described as "hazarding his immense fortune, the largest in America"[2] in the cause of liberty, did not want his son to build a house as extravagant as Homewood.

Charles Carroll of Carrollton held the purse strings to an enormous family fortune accumulated over the course of three generations in Maryland: he bought the 130-acre farm known as Liliandale for his newlywed son in 1800; advanced him $1,500 for its improvements; and fixed him for all else with an astronomical allowance of $5,000 per year. Why build a large, new house on a farm already equipped with adequate buildings, reasoned the business-minded Carroll, when in due course his own palatial country seat, Doughoregan Manor, would devolve upon young Charlie?

Footnoting the elder Carroll's practicality was the knowledge that his own father would have disapproved of the undertaking. Charles Carroll of Annapolis observed Edward Lloyd's extravagant completion of Samuel Chase's Annapolis town house in 1771 and wrote son Charles Carroll of Carrollton, "Were Lloyd my son I should not like his

Charles Carroll, Jr., probably designed his elegant, compact country house, Homewood, with the help of carpenter-builder William Edwards and design books of the period. The project required funds in excess of $40,000 for which Carroll tapped his wealthy father, Charles Carroll of Carrollton. Carroll, Jr.'s, personal life was ruined by alcoholism, but his house endured miraculously intact through private ownership and public use until its restoration in 1987.

sinking £10,000 in a house."[3] By the time young Charlie was finished, he would sink $40,000 in his house.

The father's rebukes for his son's lavish expenditures continued for the duration of Homewood's construction and chronicled its growth. In February 1801, after carpenter-builder William Edwards submitted an estimate for Homewood's construction, Carroll peevishly allowed his son $10,000 for the house. By November of that year, he was complaining bitterly to his son via the post of excessive bills for horses, carriages, and furniture, but seemed hopeful, nonetheless, that "the bricklayers are discharged for the present and the carpenters are at work upon the inside of ye house."[4]

The sunny southeast room is furnished as an office with a Baltimore Federal mahogany inlaid secretary, painted floorcloth, and toile de Jouy roller-printed curtains. The simply gathered curtains were typical of window treatments in small, late eighteenth-century rooms and bedrooms.

A letter of July 1802 recommended "a constant residence at Homewood to which you might remove your family by the middle of [the following] April, by that time I hope your house will be finished and painted, and the disagreeable smell of ye paint gone off."[5] But the bills kept coming, and, by a month later, Carroll raged that he would pay no more after October.

> What an improvident waste of money—You are imposed on by an undertaker, who leads you into extravagant expenditure . . . The time will come when you will severely feel and deeply regret so much money thrown away on such baubles, which a want of thought or a silly pride has occasioned you to spend without consulting me.[6]

Apparently, the pangs the elder Carroll suffered at his son's irresponsibility weren't ameliorated by the sight of beautiful interiors taking shape. A vibrant polychrome paint scheme of cool-hued formal rooms, sunshine yellow corridors, and shades of green family quarters represented the cutting edge of colorful interior design practiced an ocean away by Robert Adam in London.

Expensive faux finishes fooled the eye and duplicated the effect of imported wood and stone. Pine doors were painted and grained to look like mahogany. Baseboards were marbleized to mimic Italian stone, like the deeply veined, Siena marble recreated on the dining room baseboards. Carpenters employed at the height of America's love affair with carved architectural detail labored three long years embellishing mantels, chair rails, columns, pediments, and fanlights with the delicate motifs of their trade. The plasterer's artful moldings, as well, made Homewood's unique ceiling spaces elegant, crowning achievements. Finally, most riveting: at a time when fourteen-karat gold leaf pressed between panels of glass was considered a very sophisticated furniture inlay, Carroll was commissioning an entire panel of églomisé for the fanlight over his north entrance.

Charles Carroll, Jr., moved his family to Homewood late in 1803, but the house was probably not completed until 1806 and year-round residence not undertaken until 1809. Charlie never stopped submitting bills nor did his father cease to pay. In 1805, the elder Carroll sent an order to his English agent for "floor cloths for some rooms in my son's country house near Baltimore . . . for summer's use."[7] Fancy Brussels carpets were ordered, sight unseen, from Europe as were Spode china and English silver for the table. Charles Carroll of Carrollton prefaced each handwritten directive to his agent with "the most fashionable" or "the most stylish." His floor cloth orders were even accompanied by dimensions.

By 1805, the total cost of Homewood was no less than $40,000. The monetary irritations continued, but a bigger worry beset the old man in 1810: Charles Carroll, Jr.'s, addiction to alcohol. The problem, variously attributed to the younger Carroll's lack of occupation and motivation, his belief that family and fortune excused his profligacy, and his shy wife's disinclination to entertain, led to the failure of their marriage in 1816. The Carroll and Chew families' shame was expressed by Carroll's nephew, John Eager Howard, Jr., in 1814:

OPPOSITE, ABOVE: *The delicate tracery of a shield-shaped window in the pediment of the south portico characterized architecture of the Federal period and Charles Carroll, Jr.'s, lavish attention to detail.*

CENTER: *The passage traversing Homewood's east-west axis is an architectural tour de force. Boldly carved Federal elements and arched ceilings etched in crisp plaster detailing meet in vibrant yellow and green neoclassical wall hues.*

BELOW: *Sunlight from an églomisé-paneled fanlight in Homewood's back hall spills across triple lengths of painted floorcloths. The interior fanlight over the double doors borrows back hall light to maximize the airiness of an exquisitely plastered ceiling in the passage.*

I had no conception of the selfishness and terrible want of principle . . . What will be the end of this it is impossible to say—we can't get him to shoot himself, so must bear with his degradation still longer.[8]

The degradation ended in 1825 when fifty-year-old Charles Carroll, Jr., died at a place in Annapolis run by the Catholic church where he may have been sent to dry out. Charles Carroll III occupied Homewood, but he left to live at Doughoregan Manor upon the death of his grandfather in 1832. Homewood was sold to Samuel Wyman in 1839 and eleven years later was used as a guesthouse when the Wymans sought privacy from the new extension of Charles Street by building another house on the property. The Wymans allowed the Country School for Boys to use the house as its school building beginning in 1887 and then sold it to The Johns Hopkins University in 1902. During its use as faculty club, dormitory, and offices, the house remained little altered. After its first restoration and installation as a house museum by Francis Garvin in 1930, an endowment was set up in 1973 by Robert G. Merrick, former student and trustee of the university, enabling restoration based on architectural investigation and research of family papers, inventories, and the related papers of Baltimore families in the early nineteenth century.

Nearly a decade of scholarship was undertaken after 1975 by Susan Tripp, director of The Johns Hopkins University Collections, to discover what Homewood looked like circa 1810 when Charles Carroll, Jr., lived there with his family. As soon as the deans' offices were moved out of the building in 1982, restoration was begun in earnest. Probings supervised by architect John Waite of the firm Mendel Mesick Cohen Waite and Hall of Albany, New York, revealed a structure extraordinarily sound and intact for its years and use.[9] Major repairs were only necessary to the roof, brickwork, back porch, and interior finishes.

Homewood's three beautifully proportioned public rooms on the south façade, five less-formal rooms on the north, and four chambers around a central hall at the head of a small staircase to the second floor were relieved of nearly two centuries of paint. Two paint analyses of the rooms' walls and woodwork disclosed an initial off-white coat of paint and a subsequent polychrome scheme of blue,

Candelabra without candles signify a table set for daily late-afternoon dining, as was customary in the early nineteenth century. English Spode and George III silver are typical of the fine furnishings the Carroll family ordered for their table from abroad. Charles Carroll of Carrollton, whose portrait by Rembrandt Peale hangs to the left of the fireplace, was educated in Europe, as were his children. In his lifetime, he was one of the wealthiest men in America.

pale gray, sunshine yellow, cream, five shades of green, and marbleized baseboards. The restored colors were a dazzling introduction to Charles Carroll, Jr.'s, style.

Alas, as a decade of study showed, little tangible evidence remained of Carroll's taste in furnishings. The inventory of the contents of Homewood at his death in 1825 was disappointingly insufficient as a basis to furnish the house. Harriet Chew Carroll may have taken many pieces of furniture with her when she left the marriage, bringing her female children to live with her in Philadelphia near her mother. Too, the furnishings Charles Carroll of Carrollton paid for may have reverted to him in 1825.

Voluminous research into Carroll family papers, particularly Charles Carroll of Carrollton's letters to his son and orders dispatched by him to his English agent, revealed sources for some furnishings. The outstanding Brussels carpets at Homewood were produced by the English firm Woodward and Grosvenor, from English designs, called point papers, known to have been in use the years the carpets were ordered. A portrait of George Washington attributed to Gilbert Stuart now hangs in Homewood's drawing room because a Charles Carroll, Jr., letter to his father documents him hanging his father's portrait in the same room with that of George Washington.

The lion's share of Homewood's rich and colorful installation was deduced by comparisons with the inventories of other houses of the time, especially Carroll family houses, to see what they liked in their rooms. Nearby Belvidere's inventory was closely studied because Harriet Chew Carroll's sister resided there as the wife of John Eager Howard. Shared heritage and social status could have shaped similar ways the sisters used and furnished their houses. Virtually none of the furniture, art, porcelain, and silver at Homewood are the same pieces used by the Carroll family, but everything reflects what a preeminent family of early nineteenth-century Baltimore could have ordered on unlimited funds to fashionably furnish its country house.

Homewood's public debut in 1987 represented the culmination of a major phase of restoration, but the work is not finished. As new sources are found helping document the house's use and furnishings, the installation will change to reflect that scholarship. Homewood, the National Historic Landmark and museum of nineteenth-century decorative arts and architecture, is moving gracefully toward the beauty its owner and builder envisioned in 1801.

ABOVE: *The only furnishing in Homewood attributed by legend or documentation to have come from Homewood is the "Homewood Chair" (under right window). The family who formerly owned it was told the painted armchair with the lion medallion came from the house.*

BELOW: *The drawing room has been called the best-documented room for the close association its furnishings have with the Carroll family. The circa 1800 set of painted arm- and side chairs was purchased by a friend of Charles Carroll, Jr.'s, whom Carroll accompanied to New York when the furniture was purchased. The English-made Brussels carpet, like several others in the house, is of a pattern and vibrancy known to have been available in 1805 when Charles Carroll of Carrollton ordered wall-to-wall, hand-loomed carpet from England for his son's house.*

*In keeping with the spirit of the Quakers who
built the house, the Talbot County Historical
Society maintains a spare approach to its
furnishings.*

We tenderly exhort all, seriously to consider plainness and simplicity . . . and to manifest it in their speech, apparel, furniture, salutations and conversations.

—Philadelphia Yearly Meeting Discipline, 1806

Neall House

Quakerism was more than a century and a half engrained in Maryland life when James Neall built his brick house in Easton. Charles Calvert's seventeenth-century invitation to the persecuted Quakers to settle in Maryland produced some far-reaching effects, not the least of which was the architecture of Neall's house.

Plainness and simplicity—the tender exhortations of Neall's religion did not urge for its adherents an architectural aesthetic of "less is more"; nevertheless, plainness and simplicity are manifested in the three-and-a-half-story town house Neall built on South Washington Street between 1804 and 1810.

Since the Talbot County Historical Society purchased the Neall House in 1956 and restored it in 1962, the building's spare beauty has more than justified its existence. Its Federal style is not only graceful after the ponderous ostentation of the earlier Georgian style but also uncommonly practical and functional for being filtered through the Quaker sensibility. As a result, the Neall House is a distinctive example of Federal architecture in a town which flourished and produced much fine architecture between 1780 and 1830.

Three bays wide by two rooms deep, the tall, narrow structure, with the two-story rear wing added between 1820 and 1830, after Neall's occupancy, has a number of notable elements in its design: The Flemish bond brickwork of the front façade exhibits raised mortar joints, a difficult masonry technique imparting greater uniformity and finish to the important street side of the house. Where fanlights over entrance doors were usually semicircular and ornate in the Federal period, the Neall House has a plain, five-pane transom over the entry door. The molded brick cornice on the front façade has exceptionally fine detail. Parapet gables ornament the roof ends. Sandstone keystones with reeded surfaces project from handsome splayed stone lintels over the door and window openings.

Inside, the side hall plan on the first floor is typical of

ABOVE: *Fine workmanship on the house extends to the masonry of its exterior walls. The north side of the building was uniformly finished in a random common bond, but the front façade was treated to raised mortar joints for a polished presentation to the street.*
BELOW: *A rear door exited to the working yard where a smokehouse, milk house, stable, carriage house, shed kitchen, plank shed, and necessary were located. The Nealls were self-sufficient on their town lot.*

houses of the period relegated to narrow building lots. Practical Quaker ingenuity would have influenced the allocation of space: the slender side entry hall is just wide enough for circulation; the staircase favors function rather than display; and the adjacent double parlors are usefully large and well proportioned.

The staircase, confined as it was to the southwest corner of the house, enabled one large (possibly family bed-sitting) room to engulf the front half of the house and a smaller chamber to take up the northwest corner. Third-floor and attic rooms probably served as bedchambers for Neall's children and apprentices in his business. In all, ten rooms (eight with fireplaces) compose the three-and-a-half-story house and the rear addition. A fireplace in the cellar probably functioned for cooking until the rear wing with its ground-level kitchen was added.

The plans for the Neall House possibly originated in the first pattern book of architectural prototypes published in America. Asher Benjamin's *Country Builder's Assistant*, published in Baltimore in 1797, contains plans for a Federal town house similar to the plan for the Neall House. The likelihood of James Neall procuring and using such a book is great considering he inherited his brother's cabinetmaking business in 1800 and would have had the means, social standing, and professional interest to want to undertake such a house. Too, his Quaker orientation did not discourage building a big, handsome house. Wealth and the manifestations of it were not abhorred in Quaker circles if the owner were honest, hardworking, and living within his means.

The Nealls were a respected family on the Eastern Shore whose presence in Talbot County predated the construction of the Neall House by 130 years. Four generations of Francis Nealls had acquired and worked the land, the first of that name being twelve years old in 1661 when he was indentured to his uncle in Annapolis following his parents' death in a shipwreck between New England and Barbados. The 1,000 acres Francis Neall I purchased in Talbot County between 1679 and 1711 devolved upon a large number of descendants, but so industrious were they that the custom of primogeniture never reduced younger sons to penniless dependents.

Joseph Neall, the second son of Francis Neall IV, built a dwelling house, cabinetmaking shop, and additional out-

The Federal period architecture of the Neall House is uncommonly practical and monumental for having been filtered through the Quaker sensibility of its owner-builder, James Neall.

buildings on lot number 116 in Easton circa 1797. He was considered a member of the upper middle class, and his prosperous cabinetmaking business included clients from the wealthy Lloyd, Tilghman, Hollyday, and Goldsborough families. When he died in 1800 at the age of forty-four, he bequeathed to his twenty-three-year-old brother James "all my right title and interest of the lot on which I now dwell and with all the improvements thereon and thereunto belonging" which, with the tools of his trade he passed along, were worth at least $1,649.71.

James Neall married a Quaker girl, Rachel Cox, in 1801 and started building in 1804 his large brick house next to Joseph's cabinetmaking shop and former home on South Washington Street. Seven dependencies—smoke house, milk house, stable, carriage house, shed kitchen, plank shed, and necessary—would eventually fill the working yard behind the Washington Street buildings.

During the estimated six-year construction period of the house, Neall supported his wife, five children, and as many as eight apprentices who, according to Quaker discipline, were treated as family members. (The Neall children

A dearth of furnishings in Neall House underscores the Quaker simplicity of its design. The family bed-setting-room on the second floor features no fancy cornice and just the plainest of fireplace mantels.
RIGHT: *Spacious, well-proportioned, and enhanced with mahogany-grained double doors, the double parlor afforded its owners first-floor dining and entertaining facilities.*

eventually totaled thirteen with six living to adulthood.) The apprentices came and went in the Neall household, as many as fifteen between 1804, when the Nealls started the house, and 1817, when they moved out. They probably slept dormitory style in the attic, and their duties included furniture production and household chores as well as attendance at Quaker meeting. Cabinetmaker John Needles, whose fine work is today displayed in the Baltimore Museum of Art, apprenticed five years with James Neall in Easton before establishing his successful shop in Baltimore.

A measure of James Neall's own success, at least by modern standards, was not only his house and business: The tax records of 1817 ranked him thirty-fifth in real property out of 353 people in Talbot County. He had a significant investment in his cabinetmaking business which produced mostly pine case furniture such as chests, tables, desks, and clock cases. He was also preeminent in the community, serving as executor and appraiser of several estates, as an original stockholder of the local bank, and as chairman of the antislavery committee of his local Quaker meeting. By 1818, however, Neall had closed his cabinet and joiner business and moved to nearby Chancellor Point in Talbot

The operation of a cabinetmaking business from the house included the care and feeding of as many as eight apprentices at a time. Meals for the large Neall family and workers originated in this small, brick-floored kitchen.

County to be a farmer, possibly a gentleman farmer. He had exchanged his entire Easton property for Woosley Manor, owned by Jabez Caldwell. The property exchange was valued even at $9,000 by the two men and traded for $1. In 1820, probably because of a major agricultural depression, Neall quit farming and once again took up furniture making. Advertisements in the 1820s Easton newspapers indicate he was displaying ready-made furniture to the public in an Easton "wareroom" rather than contracting with individual clients.

James Neall's career took a downward turn when he left

A narrow front hall behind the entry is one's introduction to the ascetic Neall House. Beyond the archway is another hall with a staircase and a closet. Rosehead wrought nails discovered in the closet's construction helped date the house to the pre-1815 advent of machine-made nails.

the big house he built in Easton. He sold his last piece of Talbot County property in 1830 and at the age of fifty-five moved to Philadelphia to train under his cousin, Daniel Neall, as a dentist. He returned to Easton in 1839, a dentist, and hung his shingle across the street from his former home. He died in 1841, and two of his daughters opened a millinery shop in his dental office.

One must wonder how Neall felt about the financial reverses he experienced after he relinquished his South Washington Street house, and how he felt when he returned to Easton only to look across the street every day at the fine brick house he built and owned in earlier days. Certainly, the Neall House did not fare any better after the Nealls left. Jabez Caldwell lived there one year before he rented it to tenants. At least five subsequent proprietors turned a profit by renting the property. When the Talbot County Historical Society purchased the building from the estate of Dr. Stevens, the Neall House was slated for demolition. A parking lot was to take its place.

The Neall House is a fine example of Federal town house architecture influenced by the most current design type of its day and by the practical orientation of its Quaker owner-builder. Its relevance to Easton history includes its ties to the local Quakers whose industry influenced Easton's growth: Twenty years before it was built, the fledgling town of Easton contained only six families. The Neall House is situated within the National Historic District of Easton, designated in 1976.

One morning in the spring of 1986, a pane of glass nearly two centuries old fell out of the Palladian window in the south façade of Poplar Hill Mansion. It landed with a thump on the lawn two stories below. It didn't break. The thick, wavy glass didn't even crack. Workmen puttied it back in place the next day.

In 1860, a city-wide fire destroyed the old town of Salisbury and most of its eighteenth-century architecture. Poplar Hill was one of the only early structures to survive. Twenty-six years later, fire again ravaged Salisbury and Poplar Hill Mansion was again spared: the fire was stopped four blocks from the two-story frame mansion with the lovely Palladian windows.

Lest Providence take too much credit for preserving Salisbury's oldest building, there is a cast of characters as long as its history who have played parts in insuring the status of the place. Prominent names in Salisbury's history—Winder, Handy, Dashiell, Huston—recur in Poplar Hill's history. More recently, architectural preservationists and concerned Wicomico County citizenry have pulled together to convert the private residence that had seen better days to a city landmark on the National Register of Historic Places. And then there is the mansion's last owner, Dorothy Garber, who could have sold it at great profit to a private buyer in 1974 but chose instead to sell to the State of Maryland for $65,000. Mrs. Garber's appreciation of the house and its fine Federal interior detailing precluded her ever altering it. A hefty cash offer once made to her for the mansion's seven original brass door locks was summarily dismissed.

To be fair, Poplar Hill Mansion's longevity is at least partially beholden to its charm. In any age, it is not a building to be taken for granted. The stately, starkly vertical building at the far end of Poplar Hill Avenue has a purity of form that stands out vividly in the suburban neighborhood that has overtaken it. The poplar trees that once lined the mansion's long access road have given way to parked automobiles, and the fields on either hand are now full of houses but Poplar Hill Mansion has lost not a whit of its former grace and dignity.

The size of the house rivets attention. Five bays wide by four bays deep, its overall proportions are reminiscent of late-eighteenth-century New England houses. The symmetrical Georgian proportions and detailing of the front

Poplar Hill Mansion

Two nineteenth-century citywide fires took most of Salisbury's early architecture. The mansion on Poplar Hill Street, built on part of a 1732 land grant, was one of the only eighteenth-century buildings to survive.

The symmetry and detailing of Poplar Hill Mansion is typical of Georgian architecture in Maryland, but its girth and proportions are reminiscent of late eighteenth-century New England.

facade, however, are characteristic of late-eighteenth-century Maryland architecture. Contributing to the building's strict Georgian formality are the steeply pitched roof, cornice articulated by a pattern of dentils and modillions, Palladian window with fluted pilasters, and narrow central door surmounted by a fanlight. Although the formula for Georgian symmetry is not rigidly adhered to in the design for Poplar Hill Mansion, the Palladian window is repeated in the north façade, and identical bull's-eye windows ornament the apex of the pedimented gables in the east and west facades.

Connoisseurs of the formal Georgian tradition in architecture can savor the generous eleven-foot-wide central passage that extends the width of the house, and the large arch in the center of the passage which is supported by fluted pilasters. But the real charm of the interior is its extensive woodwork. Wainscoting circumvents nearly every room in the house and is often finished with an elaborate hand-carved chair rail of reeded molding. Six of the mansion's large rooms have fireplaces with fluted mantels and

Another Palladian window on the landing opposite the hall illuminates to perfection the russet hues of a well-worn, New Jersey heart pine staircase.

much carved woodwork of the sort found only in the finest houses of the Federal period.

The arch in the central passage frames a wide staircase to the second floor and a portion of the handsome Palladian window on the landing. Sunlight streaming through the old window warms the staircase made of New Jersey heart pine; the well-worn, russet-hued pine is warm, informal, and perhaps the only unpainted wood surface in the house. In 1945, when Poplar Hill Mansion was purchased and restored by Mr. Frederick Adkins, the central hall and east chamber woodwork, stripped of twentieth-century paint, revealed what may have been traces of the colors original to the construction of the house. And what colors they were! Local resident Robert Withey recalls seeing the mantel and baseboards in the east chamber (in the portions where the twentieth-century paint was taken off) painted to simulate white marble; the wainscoting painted white; and the walls painted an unusual Pompeian red.

Restoring Poplar Hill Mansion to its appearance at the time of its construction continues to be no easy task. As charmed a life as destiny seems to have provided the mansion, the date of its construction and its builder are unknown. Extensive paint analysis might reveal colors more in keeping (than the current overall beige and white applied in 1974) with the period functions of the rooms, but the questions "Who built the mansion and when?" finally answered would have important stylistic implications for the site.

The mystery of who built Poplar Hill Mansion has been extensively researched in local records, patents, wills, and inventories. Tradition has it that Major Levin Handy, formerly of Rhode Island, built the house circa 1800 on 357 acres of the 1732 land grant Pemberton's Goodwill from which Salisbury Town was also subdivided. Poplar Hill's less-than-typical Maryland architecture has been explained by Major Handy's having lived in Rhode Island and been influenced by New England architectural styles. Handy's widow, Nelly, however, is supposed to have sold the property in January 1805 to Peter Dashiell for $300. Because small houses on one-sixth of an acre of land in the vicinity of the mansion were known to have been valued at $250 in 1798, it is hard to believe that property with a house the size of Poplar Hill sold for $300 in 1805.[1] Most probably, the

Wainscoting circumventing nearly every room in Poplar Hill Mansion is ornamented with the kind of carving found in the finest houses of the Federal period.

property was without the house. (In addition to the 1805 transaction, Peter Dashiell is recorded in the Worcester County land records as having bought at auction in March 1804 228½ acres of Handy's Pemberton's Goodwill land for approximately £85.)[2]

Could Peter Dashiell have built the mansion on either of the tracts he procured from Levin Handy? A brick with the date 1805 imprinted on it found in the mansion's foundation during its 1974 restoration might support the theory that Peter Dashiell built the house soon after buying the property in 1804 or 1805. But Dashiell deeded some of the property to his brother-in-law, Dr. John Huston, in July 1805. One must wonder if the six months to one year the property was in Dashiell's possession allowed him enough time to finish a house the size of Poplar Hill or time just to begin the house.

A slightly off-center Palladian window lights an ample second-floor hall. Dr. John Huston probably built Poplar Hill Mansion between 1805 and 1810.

The honor of building Poplar Hill Mansion seems to devolve by default upon Dr. Huston whose inventory at the time of his death in 1827 was ten pages long and included enough handsome worldly goods to furnish a house the size of Poplar Hill. Included in the inventory, for example, were more than fifty-seven chairs, at least four dining tables, numerous "pictures," carpets, "Toylette Tables," desks, looking glasses, and quantities of highly valued silver and china. The seventeen slaves listed could have adequately maintained for the doctor a property and house as large as Poplar Hill.[3] Stylistically, architectural historians tend to date the house after 1805 because the interior woodwork resembles "that of the period of the 1810 home of George Read in New Castle, Delaware."[4]

In the search for information on who built Poplar Hill Mansion, one cannot overlook details such as the obituary of Dr. Huston's daughter, Isabella, discovered by former Wicomico County librarian Mrs. Lucille Horsley in 1981. "Isabella Humphreys, widow of Dr. Cathell Humphreys, died at her home on Division Street, last Tuesday, June 29, 1897 . . . Isabella was the daughter of Dr. John Huston, who purchased in 1800 Poplar Hill, then incomplete. Dr. Huston completed the property and made it the family home for over 50 years."[5] Perhaps Dr. Huston finished circa 1805 the work of another man and incorporated the more fashionable Federal style interior of his own time. Until more definitive evidence is located, the most intriguing aspect of Salisbury's finest early building will be who its builder was.

It sits in the vicinity of Baltimore's Inner Harbor, near the Aquarium, the World Trade Center, and Harborplace. Its style is 1812 Federal town house, an anachronism in the surrounding chic, but an appropriate reminder that Baltimore enjoyed an earlier heyday at this very spot.

The man who lived in the Carroll Mansion probably had more to do with financing Baltimore's greatness than any man of his day or ours. Charles Carroll of Carrollton, scion of the wealthiest family in colonial America, was, in his own lifetime, the richest and most powerful individual in Maryland. He was worth a whopping $1.6 million when he died in 1832, yet his pecuniary celebrity was eclipsed during the final five years of his life by worldwide fame as the last living signer of the Declaration of Independence.

Carroll Mansion is large, perhaps the largest and finest of those magnificent in-town houses of Baltimore's merchant class that lined the streets in the early 1800s. In 1874, it was considered the finest house in Baltimore, and, as the face of the city changed, it became the only example left of a Federal residence incorporating ground-floor business facilities in the fashion favored by the city's first merchant princes.

Carroll Mansion is a survivor, right through its use as a furniture store and its misuse by vagrants sleeping in the halls. It was spared by virtue of its three-floor hanging staircase and because a century-old memory persisted that here was "where Charles Carroll died." The City of Baltimore purchased the house in 1914 as a part of the centennial celebration of the writing of "The Star-Spangled Banner," but preservation was not guaranteed until 1963 when public and private funds were finally appropriated for complete renovation.

Today, the mansion is one of the Baltimore City Life Museums (a nonprofit institution), which include the Peale Museum, the H. L. Mencken House, the 1840 House, and the Urban Archeology Center. The museum's great size and authentic Federal style highlight Museum Row on Lombard Street. Architecturally, its distinction lies in its handsome integration of practical ground-floor business facilities and elegant upper-floor living quarters. A simple marble belt course on the five-bay-wide, Flemish bond brick façade separates the practical from the elegant; but originally separate entrances also underscored the dichotomy. A Lombard Street business entrance, which was re-

Carroll Mansion

OPPOSITE: *Author Josiah Quincy took his leave of a spry eighty-nine-year-old Charles Carroll on the precipitous descent of these stairs in 1826. "On terminating my first call upon the very active patriarch, he started from his chair, ran downstairs before me, and opened the front door," Quincy wrote in his book* Figures of the Past. *"Aghast at this unexpected proceeding, I began to murmur my regrets and mortification in causing him the exertion. Carroll, in turn, was surprised at his visitor. 'Exertion!' he exclaimed. 'Why, what do you take me for? I have ridden sixteen miles on horseback this morning, and am good for as much this afternoon . . . '"*

placed by a window, served clerks, rent-paying tenants, and loan seekers who figured in Charles Carroll's financial empire. The Lombard Street main entrance, framed by a portico with Ionic columns and a wrought iron balcony, admitted Caton-Carroll family and friends. If the front entrance left any doubt about its exclusivity, a marble foyer beyond the door, with an immense hanging staircase to the upper floors, was an altogether fitting reminder that the man who lived with his daughter's family upstairs was, as Daniel Webster wrote, the "sole survivor of an assembly of as great men as the world has witnessed."

The house was not always imposing. Baltimore tax records for 1808 indicate that a small structure occupied the

site of the Carroll Mansion at the corner of Stillhouse and King George streets (now Front and Lombard streets). The foundation of that structure is thought to exist today as the twenty-foot-wide corner room in the basement. Transformation of the little building was rapid in the decade between 1808 and 1818 as improvements were made by three different owners. A northwest basement with arches and vaulted ceilings was added to support the weight of the building's increased height. Two staircases were installed. The width of the building was more than doubled to 40 feet, 11 inches; interior rooms were 15 feet, 6 inches tall. Profits realized by the three consecutive owners totaled a hefty $16,500 in the decade of the Carroll Mansion's growth.

OPPOSITE, ABOVE: *Legend attributes the use of the large third-floor bedroom and adjacent "closet" to Charles Carroll. He may have died in this room in 1832. The shield-back side chair beneath the window is the only piece of furniture in the Carroll Mansion owned by the Carroll family.*

OPPOSITE, BELOW: *The tall tiger maple and mahogany four-post in the Caton bedroom was probably made in Baltimore circa 1830. Baltimore orioles adorn the reproduction roller printed cotton canopy and the bases [dust ruffle] beneath the 1845 Baltimore album quilt. The block print wallpaper and the carpet are reproductions of early nineteenth-century French designs.*

ABOVE: *Tradition attributes the round, painted table in the parlor to America's first female professional artist, Sara Miriam Peale. The set of painted wheel-back chairs was made in Baltimore circa 1830.*

The extravagant wallpaper and elaborate draperies in the dining room are based on original designs from 1820. The Wilton carpet was woven for the room based on a nineteenth-century painting featuring interiors of a house in Baltimore. The circa 1825 Baltimore mahogany veneer sideboard displays mahogany knife boxes of 1830 and a Samuel Kirk tea service of 1824. The Magnanimity of Scipio Africanus *was painted by the Dutch artist Isaac Paling circa 1680. If this room indeed functioned as the Caton-Carroll dining room, Lafayette may have been among the luminaries invited to early afternoon dinner here with Charles Carroll of Carrollton.*

By the time merchant Christopher Deshon sold his residence *cum* business office to Charles Carroll's son-in-law, Richard Caton, the asking price of $20,000 was hardly too steep for the area or Baltimore's thriving economy. In exchange, Caton took title to an unusually large house for its period in Baltimore that would accommodate for the winter months his wife Mary, his father-in-law Charles Carroll, his daughter Emily MacTavish, her husband John, and their four children, plus numerous servants. The Caton-Carroll family made further renovations and additions so that the final four spacious floors, full basement, separate kitchen wing, stables, carriage house, and working yard were quite sumptuous, presaging the likes of New York City's Astor and Vanderbilt abodes. One complete floor of the mansion was reserved for formal entertaining; a fourth-story attic provided sleeping quarters for the children; and the street level incorporated an office with its own vault for the storage of valuables. Such a residence could create quite a splash for its new owners.

Richard and Mary Caton, however, needed no introduction to the star-studded society of Federal Baltimore. Aside from Mary Carroll Caton's status as daughter of one of America's leading citizens (and his favorite child at that), she excelled in her own right as, in the words of an 1828 English visitor, "one of the most accomplished women in Baltimore, perhaps in the world . . . the most bewitching sweetness and grace mark her every word and gesture."[1] She was the mother of the "Three American Graces," Elizabeth, Mary Ann, and Louisa Caton, who took London society by storm in 1816 and eventually married England's most eligible and titled bachelors. The dashing Duke of Wellington fell in love with Mary Ann. A portrait of her, commissioned by the Duke, is presently in the collection of the Eighth Duke of Wellington.

Far from being the cynosure that the rest of his family was, Richard Caton turned out to be a businessman with a less-than-keen business sense. In 1824, forced to take drastic measures to alleviate his debt, Caton sold his town house. The buyer, fortunately, was his father-in-law, Charles Carroll. Although the purchase price was only $14,000, Carroll astutely deeded the property in trust to Mary Caton for her daughter Emily MacTavish, thus placing the valuable real estate beyond reach of Caton's creditors.

In this way the Carroll Mansion stayed in the Caton family until 1856 when Emily MacTavish gave it to the Catholic Order of the Sisters of Mercy. Of more importance, however, was the fact that Carroll would continue to live in the winter quarters he had grown accustomed to, with the family that he loved. Every fall, Carroll came to town laden with silver, servants, family portraits, and wagon loads of furniture mustered from his family estate, Doughoregan Manor. Originally he was not pleased with his return to the city, merely acquiescing to his daughter's wishes that he move with them for the winter into the luxurious harborside house. At eighty-one, he had developed

The mammoth Federal town house residence of the Caton-Carroll family during winters in the early nineteenth century fronted Baltimore harbor and incorporated ground-floor business facilities for Charles Carroll of Carrollton's financial empire. Son-in-law and business manager Richard Caton originally owned the house and accommodated Carroll's winter stays in the city.

ABOVE: *Never one to stint on books or learning, Charles Carroll purchased many expensive leather-bound volumes. Titles and editions duplicating Carroll's own books are shelved in a third-floor room that is called the library. The landscape of Thomas Jefferson's Natural Bridge in Virginia is midnineteenth century by an unknown artist.*

BELOW: *Age and heavy use have not ruined the fine lines of Carroll Mansion's hanging staircase. Recognition of its cantilevered grace and rarity, coupled with the legend that the last living signer of the Declaration of Independence died here, saved the house from destruction in the twentieth century.*

certain habits: daily twelve-mile horseback rides and early-morning head-first "plunge baths" in his specially made limestone pool in the country. Though a house in the city could offer no comparable opportunities for physical exercise, it was not long before Carroll was caught up in the mental stimulation of entertaining visitors from around the world.

On July 4, 1826, Charles Carroll of Carrollton acquired the distinction of being the sole surviving signer of the Declaration of Independence. The town house became a shrine. President Andrew Jackson and his cabinet came to dinner on Carroll's ninety-fourth birthday. Josiah Quincy recorded of his dinner visit that " . . . the service, though the most elegant I had ever seen, in no wise eclipsed the conversation."[2]

A twentieth-century visitor must use imagination to conjure the genteel and charming Carroll in the ambience of his past. So little of the furnishings survives from his day, and so much has happened in the interim, that his presence is just a whisper. Yet, a glance at the lofty dimensions and regal proportions of the interior tells volumes about the refinement which was his hallmark. Fortunately, the Baltimore City Life Museums have fully installed the rooms; while no one may ever know how the rooms were originally used, the furnishings accurately reflect the period between 1810 and 1832 when Carroll and the Catons lived there.

Baltimore experienced a cultural flowering during this period, and the decorative styles in the house, which range from Chippendale through Empire, are correspondingly rich and elegant. On the second floor are rooms with enormous curtain-swathed windows. The pale blue Empire drawing room dwarfs its contents: a pair of mahogany Classical Revival chairs with gothic backs, an English gilt and crystal chandelier, and a Grecian horsehair sofa. The adjacent dining room is a blaze of red and green. The bold rose-patterned Wilton carpet was woven especially for the room, its design taken from a carpet in the background of an 1826 painting of children in a Baltimore house on Albemarle Street. Expensive leather-bound books fill the small library. Carroll's collection was built over a lifetime, and reflected his view that money couldn't be better spent than in the purchase of valuable books.

The third and fourth floors were off-limits to all but the family's intimate friends. Carroll probably occupied the

largest bedroom on the third floor. From his windows, he could watch the boats in Baltimore harbor. He often entertained friends in his bed-sitting-room, which prompted the observation from visitors that he had more company than anybody in Baltimore. In the last year of his life, Carroll watched a festive procession honoring the centennial of the birth of George Washington parade below his bedroom window. Nine months later, on November 14, 1832, he died quietly in his bed in the mansion at the age of ninety-five. His body was laid out in the drawing room, and hundreds of Baltimoreans filed past to pay their last respects.

On occasion, the Carroll Mansion holds a candlelight tour, and its rooms, which in daylight seem staid simulacra of Baltimore design at its zenith, take on new life. Candlelight animates the stillness, softening the formal lines of history, and a passage from a diary written 150 years ago comes to mind: "It was night; wax lights were on the table, and a clear fire blazed on the hearth. The old gentleman, dressed in a dark purple gown, and seated in a highbacked chair, was rather of short stature, and stooped under the burden of years; his nose was aquiline, and his expression was particularly mild and engaging . . . "[3]

Ladew Manor House

None of the great houses on Maryland's roster of historic landmarks is so inextricably tied to the personality of its former owner as the Harvey Ladew Manor House in Monkton. Certainly, the preservation of the house immediately following his death in 1976 guaranteed the full impress of the man. But Harvey Ladew's inimitable style and decorating genius were bound up in the building's structure and design long before he died. His Pygmalionlike transformation of the simple Harford County farmhouse might be said to have commenced, appropriately enough, with the headline that announced his purchase to the world:

BUYS MARYLAND FARM

Harvey Ladew Is Expected To Start
Large Stable Near Belair

Special to The New York Times October 4, 1929

Baltimore, Oct. 3—Harvey Ladew of Brookville, L. I., owner of a string of valuable hunters, whose horse Ghost was ridden by the Prince of Wales for hunting in the United States, has become a landowner near Belair, Md.

Few scions of New York's Gilded Age could boast a headline in *The New York Times* for simply changing their address. In 1929, there was only one—and he was one of a kind.

Harvey Smith Ladew once threw a party where ponies were installed in the dining room munching oats from silver buckets. For another party, famed New York interior designer Ruby Ross Wood "did over" every room in the downstairs of his Long Island house; then Ladew arranged for an orchestra in the living room, a guitar player in the kitchen, and accordion music on the terrace. "I was born with a silver spoon in my mouth," Ladew once said. "Later in life I've regretted that it had not been made in the reign of one of the Georges. It was a perfectly nice spoon, however, from Tiffany's . . ."[1]

When Harvey toured Europe as a boy, he included its royal thrones—he'd make a dash for the seat when the tour guide left the room. "By the time I was fifteen," he loved to relate, "I had sat on more thrones than all of Queen Victoria's vast clan put together."[2] When Ladew wanted to

Ladew parlayed his interior design sense into a grand exterior scheme for topiary gardens that are today world famous. An allée from the house leads down to a great bowl containing an oval pool with a fountain in its basin.

ABOVE: *The Hammond-Harwood House in Annapolis was the inspiration for a drawing room Ladew made of two adjoining rooms in the old farmhouse. His rooms remain as he installed them, a mélange of style and comfort.*

BELOW: *For a man accustomed to seating one hundred in the dining room of his Long Island residence, the limitation of eight that he imposed on dinner parties in Maryland indicates how he curtailed his style to accommodate his house. The dining room was formerly the two-hundred-year-old kitchen and primary structure of the house.*

come home to enlist for World War I, he took the only boat out of Europe he could find—Kaiser Wilhelm's confiscated yacht.

He crossed the Arabian desert with a Bedouin caravan (sleeping in his dinner jacket when the wind whipped through his tent), had a mouse named for him at 16,000 feet in the Andes Mountains (*Thomasomysladewii*), lunched with Colette and Cocteau in Paris, hunted stag in France, fox in England, bighorn sheep in the American West, and retired, around the ripe age of twenty-seven, before he'd even begun to work.

Given his penchant for the limelight, his move from New York to the hinterlands of Maryland was startling. The defection, however, came as no surprise to his cronies in the Meadowbrook Hunt Club of Long Island, several of whom had preceded Harvey to Harford County, Maryland's mecca for fox hunters. The country seats they established were massive chunks of woods and farmland devoid of paved roads and barbed-wire fences. The Harford Hunt, on which they expended their considerable appetite for riding to the hounds, was modeled strictly along English lines and was one of the oldest in the country.

Small wonder, then, that soon after renovating a bungalow for himself on the grounds of the hunt club, Harvey Ladew was casting about for something more permanent. He cast no farther than the 400-acre farm next door. A prosperous family of farmers, the Scarffs, had lived there since the latter 1700s. Their silver dollar, dated 1847, replaced the "mortgage button" on the newel post of the staircase, betokening the house's paid-for status. Harvey Ladew, however, was not entirely charmed. "The farmhouse that came with the land was anything but a prize," he said, "but I couldn't pass up the promise of excellent hunting practically at my front door. I never intended to live in it but someone asked to rent my house on Long Island so I began to think about fixing up the farmhouse . . . I never moved back to New York."[3]

Ladew's dismay with the farm centered on the condition of the house and its overgrown acreage. The frame farmhouse had been constructed in two stages: The central two-and-a-half-story, three-bay section was built in the early to midnineteenth century while the two-story, three-bay hyphen on the south containing the original kitchen dated to the latter eighteenth century. A slave quarters still stood

Painted glass lunettes descriptive of the hunt complement the low-ceilinged cosiness of Ladew's "office."

The little touches that were distinctly Ladew are multifaceted. At the back of the house, a bay window with gothic style casements complements lovely gardens.

in the backyard when Harvey took the plunge and bought the property in 1929.

Probably close to the end of his first decade in the house, Ladew added the two-story, three-bay hyphen and two-story, two-bay library wing to the north end of the house. He transformed the house outwardly with gardens and inwardly with distinguished decor. Where eight rooms had answered most comfortably the needs of the former residents, fifteen distinctively designed and furnished interiors ultimately satisfied the forty-three-year-old bachelor Ladew. He once confided to a friend, "I could be happy in a house with rush furniture as long as I could have with me a few paintings and some curiosities that I really thought were fun."4 The manor house is a testament to the man's genius for interior design that sacrificed not a whit to trends and tenets and that revered comfort, pleasure, and fun above all else.

The transformation of farmhouse to manor house began immediately with two adjoining rooms in the central section which New York architect and friend James O'Conor advised be made into one large drawing room. The architectural details on the mantel, cornices, and overdoors, and the buff color of the walls were copied from a room in the Hammond-Harwood House.

On the other side of the wide stair hall in the central section, a small room was unconventionally paneled in chestnut barn siding, outfitted with a bar (behind one barn door), and called "the office." Typically, Ladew's most daring departures from the decorating norm were his most successful and always the result of some wonderful escapade. In the case of the barn paneling, a fox-hunting companion, Bryce Wing, had spotted a rare white wisteria growing on a barn in Harford County. Armed with Harvey's permission to bargain for the vine ("Buy it for me," said Ladew. "Everyone thinks I have too much money."), Wing discovered that the farmer would only sell the wisteria if the barn went with it. The wisteria, you see, was holding the barn up. "Buy it all," directed Ladew.5 Reputed cost: $17,000. Today, the rare white wisteria flourishes on a large tree near the house, and the barn timber not put to use on the estate was made into a series of nearby horse jumps called the Ladew Raceway.

The large brick fireplace and original crane were retained when the old kitchen in the south hyphen was con-

verted into an intimate dining room. The walls were painted deep yew green, and a handpainted mural of an eighteenth-century hunt, painstakingly removed from an antique French screen, was stretched on the wall between the two windows. When the screen didn't quite fill the space, Ladew himself skillfully painted six extra inches of scenery. Of Ladew's delight in using strong, unusual colors such as yew green, aubergine, and Wedgewood blue (to match a favorite pottery mug), designer Billy Baldwin has said that the English for centuries used deep, often lacquered colors regardless of unevenly plastered walls. Baldwin, a frequent guest at the manor house, attributes Ladew's inspiration for his comfortable country retreat to the English country house.

Off the dining room, a new kitchen was built and a perpendicular hyphen added to connect the kitchen with the old slave quarters out back. As subtle, witty, and constant as Ladew's humor was, it should come as no surprise that the quarters were renovated to accommodate the servants.

The hyphen and wing added to the north end of the former farmhouse changed its appearance dramatically. The oval library, Elizabethan Room, and second-story bedrooms composing the additions balanced the extant wing to the south, and the effect, while not exactly Palladian, lent a certain sophistication. The rooms are among the most beautiful and originally conceived of their time.

The oval library is the jewel of the house. It was built at the suggestion of a friend to be the setting for a single piece of furniture: a Chippendale partners' desk which Ladew brought from England and couldn't assimilate into any other room in the house. The ovoid shape of the room, its arched windows, and a half-round hunt table gracefully reiterate the oval shape of the centrally placed mahogany desk. A collection of nearly 3,000 books, what Ladew called his "circulating library," fills floor-to-ceiling shelves around the room. The eighteenth-century unpainted pine doorway was purchased by Ladew in England for the extraordinarily low sum of $300.

The Elizabethan Room, however, is Harvey Ladew at his eclectic best. The mellow paneling on the walls, found on one of his many antiquing forays into the English countryside, came from a fifteenth-century Tudor house. The elaborate ceiling plasterwork in the Tudor Rose motif was executed by New York artisans and the stone around the windows by Harford County masons. After Ladew saw the brilliant white ceiling for the first time, he immediately "aged" it by closing the chimney flue while a fire blazed on the hearth, to let the soot darken the plaster.

All through this fabulously full and creatively designed house, a theme of the hunt prevails to knit together its wealth of paintings, figurines, furniture, shadow boxes, clocks, and mementos. Fifteen rooms are united by a horse, hound, and fox motif which appears on virtually every object imaginable. Never overpowering or fatuous, the hunt is artfully and playfully displayed. "People who collect things are apt to go haywire," Ladew admitted.[6] And fox hunters, one might add, are a notoriously dedicated lot. But despite living with the sport year-round, Harvey Ladew never got enough of it.

He hunted for twenty-one consecutive seasons in England, once setting a record for hunting on both sides of the Atlantic within seventy-two hours. He hunted with the Prince of Wales: ". . . one of the six hardest riders on the English hunting field . . ." He hunted with the future George VI: "a far better horseman than his brother but by no means as bold."[7] He published articles about fox hunting in British and American journals. When he sold his hunter "Ghost" for a whopping sum following the Prince of Wales' touted ride, word crossed the Atlantic posthaste.

A ceiling like a spider's web in the Elizabethan room is actually plaster molded in the Tudor Rose motif to carry through the period ambience of the fifteenth-century pine paneling Ladew brought to Maryland intact from England.

"Harvey," chided His Royal Highness when they met at a London nightclub, "I think you owe me a commission."[8]

By far the most enterprising manifestation of Ladew's love of the hunt was his topiary. Hacking back to his quarters following a fox hunt in England, he saw a topiary horse, hounds, and fox atop Lady Sophie Scott's high yew hedge. Soon after, he was ordering topiary frames from England and growing his own fox hunt in yew on Long Island. When he moved to Maryland, he paid local farm help $1.50 per day to reshape the hillside with horsedrawn blades and drags for a serious garden. He uprooted his topiary on Long Island and planted it in Maryland.

Topiary was the seed that started Ladew's celebrated gardens and grew to encompass twenty-two acres with fifteen individual gardens. Forty-two years of his energy and ingenuity created what the Garden Club of America cited

The fox hunt, which brought Ladew to Maryland in 1929, inspired him to grow on his side lawn the yew topiary figures of a pack in full cry. The years it took to train bushes into topiary figures was worth every bit of the enjoyment Ladew derived from seeing them in his gardens.

as "the most outstanding topiary garden in America." With the help of a few part-time assistants, he worked in his old age eight or ten hours a day on his gardens. "He moved," remembered a friend, "with a sort of dogged rhythm, carrying on a low, rumbling monologue . . ."[9]

In 1965, Ladew set up a foundation for the maintenance of the house and gardens for the benefit of the public. He asked friends to serve on its board and a decade later the house and gardens were placed on the National Register of Historic Places. He added an endowment sufficient for the upkeep of the gardens and house but stipulated that there be some public support. ". . . I must be assured," he said before he died, "that the public's response will justify this disposition of my property. Otherwise, it should be bulldozed and made into something else and the proceeds given to charities . . ."[10] Today, the Ladew Topiary Gardens Foundation insures that the house and grounds not only are maintained for the enjoyment and education of the public but also preserve the genius of its bon vivant former resident.

Harvey Ladew once joked that he would live until he was seventy-five because he had enough money to last that long. But in a rare moment, he admitted that a life of pleasure, to be lived successfully, had to be taken seriously and creatively. When he died in 1976 at age eighty-nine, he had surpassed himself.

Billy Baldwin, the great American interior designer, expressed what Evergreen House meant to a generation of Baltimoreans exposed to culture within its rooms. "The gates of Evergreen opened up a whole new world to me," he wrote in *Billy Baldwin Remembers*. "There I met many internationally celebrated people; there I was surrounded by the best art and music, as well as conversation. I knew I could never return to the life I had led before."[1]

Evergreen House was the personification of culture in its heyday in the early part of the twentieth century. Ascending the carriage road on the sylvan hillside above Charles Street, one can yet see how this embodiment of classical ideals promulgated the arts so effectively in its time. The handsome rise of stone steps, four heroic Corinthian columns, and full Classical entablature of its regal portico suggest Greek perfection: Olympus, mythological home of the gods, or, at the very least, a hilltop temple to the muses.

While hyperbole best suits its past, however, erudition serves its present. Flanked by two Baltimore institutions of learning and owned by a third, Evergreen endures as a major force in the educational and cultural life of Maryland. The Johns Hopkins University was given the house and its collections in a bequest by the last owner, John Work Garrett, in 1942, and today offers students and scholars access to some of the loveliest architecture, interiors, art, and rare books in the country.

The origins of this three-story house are not definite, but its Classical Revival style and its orientation to face the then brand-new Charles Street, opened in 1850, indicate an early 1850s construction date. Stylistic parallels to the Mount Vernon Place work of nineteenth-century Baltimore architects Niernsee and Neilson also support a circa 1850 date. More concrete evidence, however, are Baltimore County maps of 1850 showing the William Broadbent family, local merchants and brokers, owning the property, fifty acres of inherited proprietary land grants. According to the Baltimore City Directory of 1860, they lived at "Glen Mary, Charles Street Avenue."

If Glen Mary was the first manifestation of the house that became Evergreen, it provided an impressive nucleus—with its simple, nearly square floor plan and magnificent two-story portico at the front façade—for later ad-

Evergreen House

The full classical entablature and graceful Corinthian columns of Evergreen's regal portico suggest Greek perfection—a mythological home of the gods or a hilltop temple to the muses.

ditions. The Broadbents' architectural taste, characteristic of Baltimore's prosperity before the Civil War, provided, also, a fabulous springboard for the coming industrial aristocracy to display their wealth.

The estate changed hands five times before the name Evergreen appeared on Baltimore City maps. Then, in 1878, the same year that Robert Garrett and Sons purchased the house, a lithograph was made showing the cream-colored, brick mansion atop its hill sequestered by an abundance of healthy conifers. For six years, the house remained as it had been pictured until the Garretts began the renovations and additions that all but doubled its size.

Robert Garrett and Sons was a Baltimore investment company with mercantile beginnings that supplied capital for the development of Baltimore in the nineteenth century. John W. Garrett, son of the company's founder and grandson of Scotch-Irish settlers in Cumberland County, Pennsylvania, financed the B&O Railroad with bonds underwritten by the family business and, as president of the B&O, placed the railroad at the disposal of the Union during the Civil War. No stranger to Baltimore's cultural scene, John W. Garrett introduced philanthropist George Peabody to millionaire Johns Hopkins at the Garretts' Montebello mansion. Over dinner, Peabody is said to have suggested to Hopkins that he give his money and his name to a worthy cause. Less than a century later, Garrett's grandson and namesake would donate his own considerable fortune to Mr. Johns Hopkins's university.

John W. Garrett bought Evergreen House for the use of one of his sons, twenty-nine-year-old Thomas Harrison Garrett, a connoisseur of the arts who acquired his first Shakespeare folio while a sophomore at Princeton. It might be interesting to speculate what gave young Garrett the greater need to enlarge Evergreen: his growing sons or his growing collections. In 1885, one year after coming into possession of the house by his father's will, Garrett added a 19 × 110-foot wing on the north end containing a billiard room, gymnasium, and two-lane bowling alley connected to the main block by a dramatic archway, or porte cochère, two stories above the drive.

In the main house, Garrett installed the mansion's first bathroom for $2,360, complete with a fireplace, gleaming solid brass fixtures, and floor-to-ceiling tesselation in a motif reminiscent of ancient Crete. His colossal book collec-

OPPOSITE: *Evergreen House was the gift of former B&O Railroad President John Work Garrett to his son in 1878. The Classical Revival structure that was a cultural lodestone during two generations of Garrett ownership today preserves the rare book collections of The Johns Hopkins University.*

ABOVE: *Gleaming English brass fixtures and cabinets installed in the second-floor bathroom in 1885 created a legend locally of the "gold bathroom" at Evergreen. Thousands of hand-placed mosaic tiles compose the walls, floor, and fireplace.*

BELOW: *The fabulous Alice Garrett, who enticed Leon Bakst from Diaghilev's Ballet Russe to design her theatre at Evergreen, herself created the Victorian bedroom from old family pieces. It's said she required only one new furnishing—the voluminous drape over the sleigh bed. The Dresden china chandelier dates to 1888 when John Garrett's mother used the room as her bedroom.*

tion filled the reading room and overflowed to the walls of the second-floor hallway. When, in 1888, the Garretts added a large, new dining room on the east, the old dining room was converted to a print room for T. Harrison's extensive collection of engravings.

Baltimore architect Charles L. Carson, responsible for the additions and alterations to Evergreen House during T. Harrison's lifetime, embellished the Classical Revival structure with lavish detail that used creative, new materials like mosaic tiles and glass. After T. Harrison's death in a boating accident at age thirty-eight in 1888, a Philadelphia architect, Lawrence Aspinwall, continued the opulent High Renaissance style renovations and garnishments to the house for Garrett's widow. His design for the new north entrance, as fabulous an entry in its own way as the original portico, included a six-foot-wide pair of doors surmounted by an ethereal semicircular glass canopy. His renovations at the rear of the house included combining two piggyback second- and third-story bedrooms into one immense fourteen-foot-tall bedroom for the Garretts' son John. The unusual room, circumscribed midheight by wrought iron balconies with glass floors reputedly designed by Tiffany, was chock full of bookshelves. T. Harrison Garrett's enormous love of books, art, birds, and collecting had passed unabated to his son.

John Work Garrett's boyhood bedroom at Evergreen, with its narrow iron staircase ascending to an aerie library of personally catalogued collections, was just one manifestation of his bibliophilism. When he married Alice Warder of Washington in 1908, his wedding gift to her was Robert Louis Stevenson's own copy of Robert Burns's poems. After inheriting Evergreen upon his mother's death in 1920, his architectural renovations included the addition of a library wing for 8,000 books.

Beginning in 1901, Garrett embarked on an illustrious diplomatic career which earned him eleven European and South American posts and the respect of countless world leaders. Intermittently, he and Alice Garrett returned to Evergreen, but they did not make their home there until Garrett retired from the foreign service in 1926.

More than any individual in Evergreen's history, Alice Warder Garrett embodied the spirit of this great house. Her husband, a man of natural modesty and dignity, was its foundation, but the irrepressible Alice—hostess, artist,

musician, dancer, and patroness of the arts—was its resident muse. She initiated a kaleidoscopic transformation of old Evergreen with the north wing. Between 1921 and 1922, the celebrated set and costume designer, Leon Bakst, forsook Paris and Diaghilev's Ballet Russe to create a theatre for Mrs. Garrett. He converted the dark, varnished wood gymnasium into a stunning private arena with white plaster walls stenciled in hundreds of intricate, multicolored designs taken from Russian wooden cookie molds. He made stage settings for Mrs. Garrett's theatrical productions; he made paintings of the divine Mrs. Garrett; and when he had completed Mrs. Garrett's costumes for her opening

LEFT: *Teak paneling in the reading room frames murals by* New Yorker *magazine artist Miguel Covarrubias. The stylized murals represent John Garrett's diplomatic posts in thirty-five years of foreign service. Through the door is the thirty-three-foot-square library with a twenty-foot ceiling designed by Lawrence Hall Fowler, A.I.A., to house Mr. Garrett's 8,000 books in 1928.*

RIGHT: *A gothic staircase descends to the Tiffany entrance, so called for the elaborate semicircular glass canopy purportedly designed by Louis C. Tiffany in 1895 over the new marble entry on the north side of the house.*

Evergreen contained close to fifty rooms when John Garrett added the large walnut-paneled library at the rear of the house for the books he and his forebears amassed in their lifetimes. Behind six arched recesses covered with locked grilles are the rarest books from the collections: a Caxton of 1480; a Gutenburg; all four Shakespeare folios; atlases of the sixteenth and seventeenth centuries; and an Audubon elephant folio. The portrait of John Garrett over the fireplace is by Zuloaga.
RIGHT: *Heraldic, opulent, and gothic describe a carved and paneled mahogany staircase addition by architect Lawrence Aspinwall in 1895.*

night performance in Evergreen Theatre, he embraced his patroness's next project, the dining room.

Bakst used his favorite colors in transforming T. Harrison Garrett's print room into Mrs. Garrett's formal dining room. A strident Chinese yellow on the walls and magenta damask at the windows imparted a certain offbeat majesty to the room. Eight long, narrow Chinese paintings in gold on magenta ground dominate the decor, emphasizing the room's height. Twenty could be seated at the table, and larger parties were accommodated in the parlors. Austere and classical, the double parlors are among the original rooms of Glen Mary. They were made into one large room with neoclassical style mantels in 1941, but the long French windows still take in a view past the portico's graceful columns that is antebellum Baltimore. Between the windows, a life-size portrait of Alice Garrett by Ignatio Zuloaga captures the consummate artiste, actress, and flamboyant mistress of Evergreen's salon. Paintings by Derain, Bonnard, Vuillard, Utrillo, and Modigliani in the parlor represent Mrs. Garrett's passion for twentieth-century art and conviction that her collection belonged in a private home setting.

In 1928, the Garretts had Lawrence Hall Fowler, A.I.A., the Baltimore architect who renovated the north wing with Bakst, design a library wing. Thirty-three feet square when it was complete, the library housed not even a quarter of Mr. Garrett's books. Walls paneled in rich Italian walnut and lined to a height of eighteen feet contained the rarest and most valuable volumes in Maryland. Six pairs of arched French doors, recessed two feet into the walls, overlooked formal, terraced gardens aligned on an axis with the addition. An enormous bronze chandelier was hung from the center of the domed ceiling, and furniture was grouped everywhere within easy access to the books. The special Alice Garrett touches—a Picasso painting, a Rodin sketch, a Brady photograph of Garrett's grandfather with Abraham Lincoln on the battlefield at Antietam—accrued slowly as she unobtrusively placed surprises for her husband on tables and bookshelves.

Evergreen is a house of many rooms, each one as unique as its period, architect, and particular Garrett could produce. There is a Victorian room with the cast-off furnishings from Alice Garrett's mother-in-law. There is the genius wing where the Musical Arts Quartet resided during its annual series of concerts. There is a Far East room, garden room, reading room, and, since 1961, the Rare Book Library of The Johns Hopkins University. In John Work Garrett's will, the house and collections were left to The Johns Hopkins University and, as stipulated by Mrs. Garrett's will, the Evergreen House Foundation was established to administer to the property. In 1983, Evergreen House was placed on the National Register of Historic Places.

Nearly a century of additions and remodeling at Evergreen includes a large, formal parlor derived from side-by-side parlors in the original 1850 building called Glen Mary. John Garrett's diplomatic career brought Georges Clemenceau, Anthony Eden, and the King of Denmark, among a host of others, to Evergreen in the early twentieth century. His wife Alice Garrett's collection of French impressionist art, acquired directly from the artists through her gallery in Paris, hangs on the walls.

Framed with mortice and tenon joinery and sheathed in clapboards, Surratt House exhibits good lines and balanced proportions, a tribute to the country carpenter hired by John and Mary Surratt for the undertaking in 1852.

Surratt House

The Victorian front door is austere, and the shuttered windows exhibit half-drawn shades. Sunlight glances off the big roof and gable chimneys but does not penetrate the heavy shadows in the dooryard. Although it stands at a thriving, sunny intersection in downtown Clinton, Mary Surratt's somber red house stands apart.

Events in history have stigmatized this midnineteenth-century clapboard farmhouse so that visitors seldom see beyond its macabre significance as the home of a woman hanged for her part in the Lincoln assassination. With every tour, Mary Surratt's tragic tale takes center stage, imparting a burdensome, brooding aura to the ten-room dwelling house and tavern.

The tavern keeper swore under oath Mary Surratt spoke to him by the woodpile. "Have the shooting irons ready," was her alleged message. The parcel she entrusted to him: field glasses allegedly intended to aid John Wilkes Booth in his getaway from Ford's Theatre. The evidence along with the shooting iron found in a wall of the house sent Mrs. Surratt to the gallows.

As thickly as the shadows hover around the building, however, its preservation entails far more than the story of a convicted criminal. A bronze plaque on the site of the fateful woodpile assures us there is no greater significance here than a memorial to an infamous deed and the first woman executed for conspiracy by the federal government:

> The Mary Surratt House built in 1852 for the family of John and Mary Surratt. Restored in 1975 to honor Mary Surratt, a victim of the hysteria following the assassination of President Abraham Lincoln.

The citizens of Clinton believed Mary Surratt innocent more than a century after she was executed. Sensationalism and tourist revenues offered no enticement to the people of this southern Prince George's County town who refused to remove the name Surratt from the local election district and who continue to use the name on roads, schools, and businesses. Under the auspices of the Maryland-National Capital Park and Planning Commission, they restored the building as a tribute to Mary Surratt's character and the good name of Surratt, respected in that area since the seventeenth century.

Surratt hotel guests were served in a small public dining room adjoining the tavern room. Spare, utilitarian furniture, inexpensive ironstone dishes, and bone-handled flatware describe a basic business enterprise. After John Surratt died, Mary moved to Washington, D.C., where she operated a boardinghouse and began her fateful association with John Wilkes Booth.

Recently, a more subtle and valuable reason has surfaced for the continuing preservation of the Mary Surratt House. What the bronze plaque does not explain and what Mrs. Surratt's notoriety tends to obscure is the fact that the house, in and of itself, merits preservation. The two-story, forty-by-thirty-two-foot rectangular dwelling of simple frame construction with two porticoes at the front and the rear is an example of mid-Victorian vernacular architecture. As such, it illuminates the all-but-forgotten milieu of everyday life around Civil War time in America.

The house is both unusual and educational, for few historic sites are dedicated to this period or this class of people. The Surratt House furnishings and lifestyle are those of an upwardly mobile family of the 1850s and 1860s. Neither landed gentry nor dirt farmers, this family was in the vanguard of America's emerging middle class, and their house represents the possibilities for social and economic improvement available to this new class of Americans. Architecturally, the building is commodious and its "lines and proportions . . . appear to be balanced and represent considerable control having been exercised by its builder . . . The net effect is one of being almost a classical quality typical to some late eighteenth century houses in Maryland."[1]

The house has much to teach about the rise of an average man, John Harrison Surratt, from subsistence-level farming to a position of local importance. A farmer who improved himself by trading properties to increase his holdings, Surratt amassed over 1,000 acres in his lifetime. He was an entrepreneur who took risks for the sake of profit. He married seventeen-year-old Mary Elizabeth Jenkins in 1840. Twelve years and three children later, Surratt acquired 287 acres of farmland at a crossroads ten miles east of Washington, D.C. In the spring of 1852, Surratt agreed to pay carpenter Jeremiah Townsend approximately six hundred dollars to build a house on the corner of the property at Piscataway and New Cut roads. In nine months, he held a tavern license. Two years after that, by an act of the Maryland General Assembly, his hotel in the house became the official polling place for the newly created Ninth Election District of Prince George's County, dubbed "Surratt's Election District."

Right on the heels of the Maryland Legislature, the U.S. Post Office Department designated the hotel a post office, and the boom at the crossroads became known as Surrattsville.

Today, the Surratt House is less than a block from the heart of Clinton's business district. Heavy equipment rumbles, unseen, on a lot to the rear; gas stations and fast-food concessions do a brisk business at the crossroads; and two regional newspapers operate from the business center up the street. Starkly old-fashioned, the Surratt House is an oasis of calm on its acre of rural property. However much as it now looks like a stubborn survivor engulfed by urban sprawl, John Surratt's house *cum* hotel was formerly the lifeblood of the town. A glance inside the door on the shed-roofed porch at the north end dispels any doubt about the building's early significance.

Not five steps from the threshold of the building's side door is a tavern counter. Above it, a sign advertises drinks for 6¼¢. Beyond it, the brick hearth of a small fireplace juts comfortably into the room. Here, in the turbulent decade before the Civil War, John Surratt's rough-clad farmer neighbors presumably came to drink and debate secession. They picked up their mail behind the tavern counter. They ate supper, for 37½¢, in the small public dining room adjoining the tavern, where Surratt's hotel guests also took their meals.

Judging from the size of the two square rooms on the first floor allotted to the public, Surratt's tavern and hotel business was small. The seven slaves he owned were probably rarely taken away from serious farm labor to serve in the kitchen and dining room. Mary Surratt and her daughter and one house servant, Rachel, probably handled the hotel chores.

Separating the public rooms of the hotel and tavern from the Surratt family quarters on the first floor is a seven-foot-wide center hall which gave the family access to the front entrance door. Toward the rear of the hall is a stairway to the second floor which exhibits an elegance in its antebellum newels and round railing not evident elsewhere in the house. One of the few reliable references to the family's use of their home is in a letter written by son John Surratt. It merely describes his mother and sister Anna sitting in the hallway to catch the summer breezes.

The assumption that Mrs. Surratt kept a parlor in the house is based upon the few pieces of furniture that are

ABOVE: *The tavern room was a hotbed of secessionist debate and a stop on the Surratts' son John's clandestine courier route between the Confederate capital of Richmond and points north.*
BELOW: *One of the few contemporary references to the Surratt House is a letter by the Surratts' son John describing his mother and sister sitting in the stair hall, apparently the most comfortable place in the house in summer, to catch the cooling breezes. The seven-foot-wide stair hall leads to a staircase at the rear displaying an elegance not found elsewhere in the vernacular house.*

The northeast bedroom features a spool-turned Jenny Lind bed and furnishings a woman of Mary Surratt's stature would have required. The sewing machine came into use at this time.

known to have belonged to her. The fine center table and French marquetry lady's writing desk are evidence of Mary Surratt's good taste. Directly behind the parlor is the room which figured so prominently in Mrs. Surratt's conspiracy trial. Today, it is furnished as a typical Victorian dining room. In April 1865 the military tribunal which conducted the case against Mrs. Surratt noted only that one of "the shooting irons" intended for John Wilkes Booth during his getaway was secreted in the wall of "the dining room."

At this point, the history of the Surratt House becomes enmeshed in the tragic dénouement of Mary Surratt's life. No one who walks into the family dining room can miss the irony inherent in its very proper, very innocent Victorian setting. Over a century ago, federal officers chopped down a wall of this room to recover a gun. The country was in emotional chaos over the assassination of Lincoln. Forty-two-year-old Mary Surratt was about to be the first woman in American history executed by the U.S. Government.

The story of Mary Surratt's association with the cabal that planned and carried out Lincoln's assassination originates from both a family and a regional loyalty to the Confederacy. Upon John Surratt's untimely death in 1862 at the age of fifty, daughter Anna wrote: "It makes me so sorry to think that poor Pa did not live to see the glorious Banner of Southern Liberty unfurled and planted upon the shores of

Maryland—it is what he long desired."[2] Son Isaac had joined the Confederate cavalry in Texas, and twenty-one-year-old John was operating a clandestine courier service between the family hotel and the Confederate capital in Richmond.

When Mrs. Surratt, out of financial necessity, moved her family (after her husband's death) to the family's H Street property in Washington to open a boardinghouse in 1864, she and two of her children began an association with the celebrated actor John Wilkes Booth. Quite possibly, but not certainly, Mary Surratt had knowledge of Booth's and her son John's plans to kidnap the president. Meanwhile, the hotel in Surrattsville was leased to an ex-policeman, John M. Lloyd, and young John Surratt continued to use it for spy-related activities.

In April 1865 the kidnapping plan turned into an assassination plot; the extent to which Mrs. Surratt was involved, or if she had any knowledge of it at all, may never be certain.

John Lloyd's testimony that Mary Surratt drove to the hotel from Washington on April 14 to give him the message and the field glasses picked up by John Wilkes Booth that night is difficult to controvert, especially when backed by Louis Weichmann, who brought her there from the boardinghouse in Washington.

With respect to her knowledge of Booth's intent to murder the president, however, all evidence against Mrs. Surratt remains circumstantial—the accused was allowed not a word in her own defense. Despite a recommendation by five members of the tribunal that Mrs. Surratt's sentence be commuted to life imprisonment "due to her age and sex," she went to the gallows on July 7, 1865, along with three others.

Her son, who had originally brought the shooting irons to Lloyd to hide in the dining room wall of the Surratt House until they were needed, was on a courier mission in New York State at the time of the assassination. He was tried two years later by a civil court in the District of Columbia. The trial ended in a hung jury, and he was never retried.

John Lloyd—who aided Booth in his escape and foiled federal troops in their pursuit, who was drunk at the time of his conversation with Mrs. Surratt by the woodpile, and whose testimony as a state's witness helped seal Mrs. Surratt's fate—was never charged with a crime. Mary Surratt's

The parlor of the Surratt House, documented in its location through the correspondence of a family friend, was a formal retreat for the family and overnight guests of the Surratts' hotel. The Federal overmantel looking glass, rosewood melodeon, and center table with a lamp and Bible are appropriate period furnishings. The center table belonged to Mary Surratt.

Mid-Victorian vernacular architecture was the expression of a new middle class of Americans emerging in the midnineteenth century. The red frame Surratt House in Prince George's County, where Mary Surratt allegedly aided John Wilkes Booth in his flight from assassinating Lincoln, preserves the architectural milieu of an upwardly mobile family of the 1850s and 1860s.

role of courier may or may not have included her understanding of the intent of the message and the field glasses. John Lloyd readily admitted to a lapse of memory due to his inebriated condition, and condemned coconspirator Lewis Thornton Powell-Paine informed his executioner minutes before she and he were hanged, "She's innocent."

In retrospect, all that can be said for sure in the case of Mrs. Surratt is that she was condemned to die on the basis of inconclusive evidence. Her former residence and scene of her dubious crime, however, keeps a careful accounting. What's more, the site offers, as no other Maryland property on the National Register of Historic Places, a unique historical perspective on the lifestyle of the emergent middle class in rural pre-Civil War America. Ultimately, the well-preserved, period, vernacular aspects of the Surratt House may prove more valuable than its role in the events surrounding the Lincoln assassination.

The parlor is Empire; the drawing room is eighteenth-century neoclassical. The state reception room has been installed to the taste of the Federal period, and the conservatory is contemporary.

Add to this layout an eighteenth-century style dining room, a Victorian sitting room, and a ceremonial hall with a three-story flying staircase. Place the rooms in a Victorian structure remodeled in the twentieth century into a colonial revival mansion . . . voilà, the official residence of the governor of Maryland.

Despite appearances, the eclectic fripperies of two hundred years of passing fads in decorating have not come to roost in Government House. Today, more than ever before, the seven state rooms of the governor's mansion in Annapolis present a lovely, cohesive, viable face to the visiting public.

A single theme unifies the disparately furnished interiors. It's simple, and it's ingenious: From the smallest piece of mantel garniture to the most formidable antique, Government House now displays only Maryland decorative traditions in Maryland-inspired settings, and utilizes, wherever possible, Maryland-made arts, crafts, and cabinetry.

The idea is unprecedented. Only a handful of gubernatorial residences in the country open their doors for public touring, and Maryland's Government House is the only one to transform its state rooms into a showcase of Maryland arts and traditions for its citizens.

The rooms look as if they've been lifted from the American wing of an art museum. But stodgy they're not. The Baltimore-made Empire sofa with hand-carved legs still serves well after 160 years. The emerald green and yellow patterned Lozenge Directoire carpet, which was woven in twenty-seven-inch-wide strips and had to be cut, resewn together, then laid in the room just as it would have been 150 years ago, still sports no protective runner. In a manner uncommonly democratic, the furnishings remain fixed for all occasions—formal state receptions or an annual Easter egg hunt for the Maryland School for the Blind.

Before 1979, these rooms had no pertinent or permanent design focus. The residence of Maryland's governor had been moved or renovated so many times in 285 years that a paucity of original furnishings survived. Few pieces of value ever accumulated, and by 1979 castoffs composed

Government House

most of the decor. One first lady described it as "a mixture of Charles Willson Peale portraits and Ethan Allen reproductions."[1]

Since a governor's budget is never sufficient to meet the cost of reinstalling such rooms, some sort of resourceful alternative had to be devised. In January 1979 Patricia Hughes, the wife of Governor Harry Hughes, invited President of the Maryland Historical Society Leonard C. Crewe, Jr., Director Romaine Somerville, and Chief Curator Stiles Colwill to Annapolis for a tour of the mansion.

"A fascinating challenge" was the consensus. "But where are the antiques?"[2] Two period Chippendale side chairs were discovered camouflaged in the reproduction dining room suite. Twenty oriental rugs were discovered squirreled away in the attic. Three Charles Willson Peale portraits hung where they couldn't properly be seen. A rare silver service from the private quarters of the house was used so infrequently, its value had been forgotten; cleaning in the dishwasher almost ruined it.

Sleuthing, however, was not to be the primary function of the Maryland Historical Society. Mrs. Hughes needed the assistance of a professional group which would redesign the state rooms, not in a warm, personal, subjective fashion, but in such a way that Maryland's culture could be displayed and lived with. Objectivity was the key.

The Maryland Historical Society had the expertise to imprint an immutable presence on these rooms; it could lend important period furnishings from its notable collections; it could encourage donations. Most importantly, the prestigious 138-year-old institution could give the project a credibility that would assure its success.

In January 1979, the Gallery Committee of the society and the Maryland Commission on Artistic Property approved a master plan for refurbishing the state rooms. Friends of Government House, Inc., a nonprofit, tax-exempt corporation, was created to receive contributions from the private sector.

From the outset, the master plan for reinstallation was clear-cut; the actual task was another matter. Government House had been built during the 1870s in the High Victorian Second Empire style. In 1935, the mansion was renovated into a pseudo-Georgian country house. Except for some Victorian woodwork and mantels, the original character of the structure was lost.

Maryland Historical Society Curators Stiles Colwill and (Ms.) Gregory Weidman found themselves working with a Maryland landmark which had no architectural coherence. Most experts would wither at the prospects. The two took a look at the high ceilings, good proportions, and fine woodwork that existed and considered themselves lucky.

They examined the salient design characteristics of each room to determine the most appropriate style for each. In search of clues on how to furnish with historical accuracy, they delved into period design books, inventories of Maryland houses of the eighteenth and nineteenth centuries, craftsmen's accounts, and old newspaper records. The lack of any authentic interior architectural style actually proved beneficial, for the rooms were thus wide open to display every decorative tradition in Maryland's heritage.

Incredibly, in just six weeks, the state reception room made its debut. Christened the Federal Reception Room, its color, architectural detail, and reproduction seating furniture seemed suitable for Maryland's Federal period, 1790–1815. Four pieces of furniture and three paintings were added; existing furnishings were rearranged to conform to historical specifications; the modern damask window hangings were simply recut into proper Federal period swags based on Hepplewhite's design book.

If the Federal Reception Room was the most obliging make-over, the Empire Parlor, 1815–1840, must qualify as the most startling. Initially, the room started as a Victorian porch; it was remodeled in 1935 into a glorified breezeway; then in December 1979 it miraculously blossomed into one of the finest (and few) examples of the Empire style in Maryland. Its historically correct emerald green and chrome yellow colors jump before the eyes. Superb examples of Maryland furniture and several fine portraits of Baltimore's Howard family underscore Maryland's, particularly Baltimore's, cultural importance to the world after the War of 1812.

As logically as the Empire Parlor seems to flow from the adjacent Federal Reception Room, one would never guess the headaches it gave its installers. Design books were consulted to find a stylistic reference point, and when the

Greek Revival aspect of the three arched windows was settled upon, the troubles were only beginning. The voluminous curtains had to be entirely handmade. The Scalamandré silk fringe of several hundred fabric-wrapped, hand-tied wood bobbins was made by two elderly ladies whose health halted the work more than once. On top of everything else, Governor and Mrs. Hughes confessed to shock after glimpsing the freshly painted chrome yellow walls.

The room is daring, inspiring, and complete, thanks to Leonard C. Crewe, Jr. As chairman of the Friends of Government House, Mr. Crewe donated an important set of Baltimore klismos chairs and all the funds necessary for the room's reinstallation.

Government House depends upon gifts, loans, and monetary contributions from private sources. A minimal fee is all that is necessary for membership in the Friends of Government House, and a tour of the seven state rooms is free to the general public. But the needs in each period room for specific period furnishings are costly; prospective donors of antiques are encouraged to be generous. Several such Friends stepped forward anonymously during the December 1980 party given by Governor and Mrs. Hughes for Friends of Government House in the nearly completed eighteenth-century drawing room. Eight chairs belonging to Maryland's first governor, Thomas Johnson, were offered on loan and have since been given to the historical society for indefinite loan to Government House. The money for a pair of andirons and a candlestand was donated. The coup of the evening was the offer of a considerable sum to buy the Maryland-made, bellflower-inlaid card table on loan from the renowned firm of Israel Sack, Inc., of New York.

The State Drawing Room, with its eighteenth-century Annapolitan paint colors and magnificent yellow curtains dyed in France to historically correct specifications, was officially complete in January 1981. Inventories of prominent Marylanders like Proprietary Governor Robert Eden and Daniel Dulaney, a colonial landowner, were consulted to find out how the most formal rooms of an important house would have been furnished between 1770 and 1800.

The eighteenth-century style dining room adjoining the drawing room duplicates a color scheme in the Upton

Scott House in Annapolis, and its red curtains are based on a 1774 design by Thomas Chippendale. The furniture, principally Maryland-made reproductions in the Queen Anne, Chippendale, and Empire styles, reflects the local preference for such items in this century. The reproduction mahogany dining table, twenty-four chairs, and two sideboards were custom-made for Government House by the Potthast firm in Baltimore in the 1930s.

A marble mantel in the smallest state room inspired a Victorian period installation; it was one of the few architectural details of the building's 1870s construction to survive the remodeling of 1935 and, as such, offered good reason to honor Maryland decorative arts in the decade following the Civil War. Because the room's Victorian period ceiling did not survive, Chairman of the Gallery Committee Mrs. Howard Baetjer suggested the substitution of one from the Buckler House on Charles Street in Baltimore, then being completely renovated for condominium use. The highly decorative plaster motifs of the rococo ceiling were carefully removed, transported to Annapolis, and pieced together to create a design on this parlor ceiling of Government House. Opened in January 1983, the Victorian Parlor displays the height of Victorian culture in Maryland with elaborate furnishings, bold colors, and a profusion of rich patterns.

The Contemporary Conservatory, completed in July 1985, not only performs the dual functions of honoring the design precepts of Baltimore-born Billy Baldwin, "the dean of American interior decorators," and of affording the mansion a much-needed informal retreat among the state rooms, but also is the first public room in any U.S. governor's residence to display in abundance the work of its twentieth-century native artists.

In summary, the seven state rooms of Government House are superbly furnished and if not more handsome than the interiors of other gubernatorial residences across the land are certainly among the most originally conceived and implemented. Government House is one of the few governors' residences to utilize donations from the private sector. The history of the various governor's mansions in Annapolis has always been colorful, from the first building, dubbed Bladen's Folly because it was too grandiose to be finished, to the Jennings House which was touted in 1769:

"Few mansions in the most rich and cultivated parts of England . . . are adorned with such splendid and romantic scenery."[3] Featured in the November 1986 issue of *Architectural Digest* magazine, Government House has established its own uniqueness while continuing Maryland's distinguished tradition for fine living.

Author's Note:
As *Great Houses of Maryland* went to press, the seven state rooms of Government House were in the process of being reinstalled with new furnishings under the aegis of Governor Schaefer. The name of Government House has been changed to the Governor's Mansion; the advisory body replacing the Government House Trust is the Governor's Mansion Trust; and the fund-raising body formerly called Friends of Government House is now the Governor's Mansion Foundation.

Government House, the official residence of the Governor of Maryland, was built in 1880 after an earlier residence of 1740 was purchased by the United States Naval Academy in their expansion. The High Victorian building was adapted architecturally in 1935 to complement its historic neighbor, the State House, and to harmonize with the colonial milieu of Annapolis.

This chapter, in an earlier version, appeared in *Country Magazine*.
1. In the possession of the Sotterley Mansion Foundation, Inc., Hollywood, Md.
2. From the archives of Sotterley Mansion, Sotterley Mansion Foundation, Inc., Hollywood, Md.
3. National Register of Historic Places Inventory—Nomination Form, prepared by Mrs. Preston Parish, Maryland Historical Trust, Annapolis, January 1972, 4.

Sotterley

Notes

1. Certificate of Survey, 1739, Hall of Records, LG#C, 54.
2. H. Chandlee Forman, *Maryland Architecture: A Short History from 1634 through the Civil War* (Cambridge, Md.: Tidewater Publishers, 1968), 52.
3. John J. Jacob, *A Biographical Sketch of the Life of the Late Captain Michael Cresap* (Cincinnati, Ohio: n.p., 1855).
4. Francis Jennings, "Indian Trade of the Susquehanna Valley," *Proceedings of the American Philosophical Society* 110 (1966): 413.
5. Basil Sollars, *Jonathan Hager, The Founder of Hagerstown* (Baltimore: Theo Kroh & Sons, 1888).
6. Francis Jennings, op. cit.
7. William Eddis, *Letters from America,* ed. Aubrey C. Land (Cambridge: Belknap Press of Harvard University Press, 1969).

Jonathan Hager House

1. John Milner, "Schiefferstadt, A Restoration Study," prepared by the National Heritage Corporation for the Frederick County Landmarks Foundation, Inc., Westchester, Pa., December 1974, 13.
2. "Frederick's Oldest Private Home Is Well-Preserved," the Frederick *News*, Tuesday, February 24, 1959, 9.

Schifferstadt

1. Michael F. Trostel, A.I.A., *Mount Clare, Being an Account of the Seat built by Charles Carroll, Barrister, upon his Lands at Patapsco,* National Society of Colonial Dames of America in the State of Maryland, 1982, 7.
2. *Ibid.,* 8.
3. Personal communication to the author from Henry Ward, Mount Clare public education coordinator for the Baltimore Center for Urban Archeology, July 1988.

Mount Clare

This chapter, in an earlier version, appeared in *Maryland Magazine.*

London Town Publik House

Paca House	This chapter, in an earlier version, appeared in *Maryland Magazine*.
	1. *Early Maryland Poetry: The Works of Ebenezer Cook, Gent: Laureat of Maryland, with an Appendix Containing The Mouse Trap,* ed. Bernard C. Steiner (Baltimore: The Maryland Historical Society, Fund Publication, No. 36, 1900).
	2. "Records of the Hominy Club" in American Historical Records, Maryland Hall of Records, 298.
Brice House	1. Brice Account Book, p. 3, Maryland Hall of Records, Microfilm No. 1207.
	2. Anne Arundel County Original Wills, Maryland Hall of Records, Liber 34, folio 243.
	3. Brice Account Book, p. 1, op. cit.
	4. Orlando Ridout IV, "The James Brice House," Master's thesis, University of Maryland, 1978, 67.
	5. Charles Phillips and Paul Buchanan, "Report Documenting the Original Form and Evolution of the Brice House," 5 volumes commissioned in 1984 by the International Masonry Institute.
Chase-Lloyd House	This chapter, in an earlier version, appeared in *Maryland Magazine*.
	1. Charles Carroll of Carrollton to Charles Carroll, Barrister, August 9, 1771, Carroll Letterbook (1770–1774), Maryland Historical Society, MS.203.2, quoted in Rosamond Randall Beirne, "The Chase House in Annapolis," *Maryland Historical Magazine* 49 (1954): 181.
	2. Katherine Scarborough, *Homes of the Cavaliers* (Cambridge, Md.: Tidewater Publishers, 1969), 211.
	3. Charles Carroll, op. cit.
Montpelier	1. L. H. Butterfield, ed., "The Adams Papers: Part III, Servants of a Young Republic," *Life*, May 25, 1962.
	2. Robert Lewis, "A Journey from Fredericksburg, Virginia, to New York," *Maryland Historical Magazine* 53 (June 1958): 180–85.
	3. John M. Walton, Jr., and James T. Wollon, Jr., "Historic Structure Report," compiled and submitted to the Maryland Historical Trust in partial fulfillment of qualifications to receive grants, March 29, 1979, 2.
	4. Robert Lewis, op. cit.
	5. *Ibid.*
	6. William Seale, "Montpelier, Project for the Interiors," prepared for the Maryland-National Capital Park and Planning Commission, History Division, Bladensburg, Md., 1983.

This chapter, in an earlier version, appeared in *Southern Accents.*

Hammond-Harwood House

1. Jonathan Boucher, *Reminiscences of an American Loyalist 1738–1789* (Boston and New York: Houghton Mifflin Company, 1925), 65.
2. Baron Ludwig Von Closen, *The Revolutionary Journal of Baron Ludwig Von Closen, 1780–1783,* ed. and trans. with an introduction by Evelyn M. Acomb (Chapel Hill: University of North Carolina Press, 1958), 220.
3. William H. Pierson, "The Hammond-Harwood House, A Colonial Masterpiece," *The Antiques Magazine,* January–February 1977, 193.

This chapter, in an earlier version, appeared in *Maryland Magazine.*

Hampton Mansion

1. Ridgely family papers. In the library of Hampton National Historic Site, Towson, Md.
2. Charles W. Snell, *Historic Structure Report: Historical Data Section, Hampton Mansion and Gardens, 1783–1909, Hampton Historic Site, Towson, Maryland* (Denver: National Park Service, U.S. Department of the Interior, August 1980), 7.
3. Ridgely family papers, op. cit.
4. Charles Ridgely Esq to Richd Jones DR (For Oil and Sundry Colours Used on the Great House from April 4th to June 4th 1791), Ridgely family papers, Maryland Historical Society, MS.1127.
5. A[ndrew]. J[ackson]. Downing, *A Treatise on the Theory and Practice of Landscape Gardening, Adapted to North America; With a View to the Improvement of Country Residences,* with a Supplement, Containing Some Remarks about Country Places by Henry Winthrop Sargent, 6th ed. (New York: A. O. Moore, 1859), 557.
6. Ridgely family papers, op. cit.

1. Narrative from Judge Shriver derived by him from his father, David Shriver, Sr., and Joel Lightner and others. Shriver Book, 1684–1888, in the archives of the Union Mills Homestead, 14.

Union Mills Homestead

2. *Ibid.*
3. Frederic Shriver Klein, "Union Mills Homestead," booklet published by Union Mills Homestead for tourists, 2.
4. *Ibid.*
5. From Andrew K. Shriver's letters to relatives in Hanover, Pennsylvania, circa 1850, from the archives of the Union Mills Homestead (not catalogued).
6. *Ibid.*
7. Reverend Samuel S. Shriver, "The Old Homestead," *Poems for the Christian Life* (Baltimore: n.p., 1897).

Teackle Mansion   1. Letter written by Miss Elizabeth Waters to her aunt, Mrs. Josiah Bayly, in Cambridge, July 31, 1811, from a letter in the possession of the late Mrs. Henry Keating in Baltimore. Present whereabouts of the letter are unknown.

2. George Alfred Townsend, *The Entailed Hat* (Cambridge, Md.: Tidewater Publishers, 1955), 104.

3. *Ibid.*, 103–4.

4. Correspondence of Littleton Dennis Teackle to merchants in Liverpool in 1806, contracting timber business. In the possession of Olde Princess Anne Days.

Homewood   1. Chew family papers, May 5, 1800, The Historical Society of Pennsylvania, Philadelphia.

2. John H. Scarff, ed., *The Bicentenary Celebration of the Birth of Charles Carroll of Carrollton* (Baltimore: The Lord Baltimore Press, 1937), 1.

3. Charles Carroll of Annapolis to Charles Carroll of Carrollton, August 16, 1771, "Extracts from the Carroll Papers," *Maryland Historical Magazine* XIII (1918): 263–65.

4. Charles Carroll of Carrollton to Charles Carroll, Jr., November 27, 1801, Carroll family papers, courtesy of Philip Carroll.

5. *Ibid.*, July 24, 1802.

6. *Ibid.*, August 24, 1802.

7. Charles Carroll of Carrollton's Letter Book, 1771–1833, Arents Collections, The New York Public Library, Astor, Lenox and Tilden Foundations.

8. Chew family papers, February 22, 1814, The Historical Society of Pennsylvania, Philadelphia.

9. Mendel Mesick Cohen Waite, Architects, "Homewood: Historic Structure Report," Baltimore, The Johns Hopkins University (unpublished document), 1983.

Poplar Hill Mansion   1. Jacqueline F. Dianich, "The Mystery of Who Built Poplar Hill Mansion," submitted to the graduate faculty, Salisbury State College, 1970, 22.

2. Worcester County Land Records, Liber Z, folio 224–226.

3. Worcester County Inventories, 1828, Liber LPS 6, folio 29.

4. National Register of Historic Places Inventory—Nomination Form, prepared by Michael Bourne, Maryland Historical Trust, Annapolis, August 1971, 5.

5. The Salisbury *Advertiser*, Saturday, July 3, 1897, 1.

Carroll Mansion   This chapter, in an earlier version, appeared in *Maryland Magazine.*

1. Raphael Semmes, *Baltimore As Seen by Visitors 1783–1860* (Baltimore: Maryland Historical Society, 1953), 101.

2. Joseph Gurn, *Charles Carroll of Carrollton 1737–1832* (New York: P. J. Kenedy & Sons, 1932), 232.

3. Captain James E. Alexander, *Transatlantic Sketches Comprising Visits to the Most Interesting Scenes in North and South America and the West Indies; with Notes on Negro Slavery and Canadian Emigration* (London: n.p., 1833), Volume II, 259.

This chapter, in an earlier version, appeared in *Maryland Magazine*.
  1. From Mr. Ladew's papers. In the possession of the Ladew Topiary Gardens Foundation.
  2. *Ibid.*
  3. *Ibid.*
  4. *Ibid.*
  5. *Ibid.*
  6. *Ibid.*
  7. *Ibid.*
  8. Harvey S. Ladew, *Random Recollections: Vanished Years* (Monkton, Md.: Ladew Topiary Gardens Foundation, n.d.), 44.
  9. From Mr. Ladew's papers, op. cit.
10. *Ibid.*

Ladew Manor House

This chapter, in an earlier version, appeared in *Maryland Magazine*.
1. Billy Baldwin, *Billy Baldwin Remembers* (New York and London: Harcourt Brace Jovanovich, 1974), 25.

Evergreen House

This chapter, in an earlier version, appeared in *Maryland Magazine*.
1. National Register of Historic Places Inventory—Nomination Form, prepared by Nancy Miller, Maryland Historical Trust, Annapolis, June 26, 1972, 1.
2. Letter from Anna Surratt to Louisa Stone, September 16, 1862, from the collection of the Surratt House Museum, A Historic Property of the Maryland-National Capital Park and Planning Commission, Department of Parks and Recreation, Prince George's County.

Surratt House

This chapter, in an earlier version, appeared in *Maryland Magazine*.
1. Personal communication to the author from Patricia Hughes, February 1982.
2. Personal communication to the author from Stiles Colwill, February 1982.
3. William Eddis, *Letters from America,* ed. Aubrey C. Land (Cambridge: Belknap Press of Harvard University Press, 1969).

Government House